Values at Play in Digital Games

Values at Play in Digital Games

Mary Flanagan and Helen Nissenbaum

The MIT Press
Cambridge, Massachusetts
London, England

MIT Press books may be purchased at special quantity discounts for business or sales promotional use. For information, please email special_sales@mitpress.mit.edu.

This book was set in Stone by the MIT Press. Printed and bound in the United States of America.

Library of Congress Cataloging-in-Publication Data

Flanagan, Mary, 1969–
Values at play in digital games / Mary Flanagan and Helen Nissenbaum.
  pages cm
Includes bibliographical references and index.
ISBN 978-0-262-02766-3 (hardcover : alk. paper)
1. Computer games—Social aspects. 2. Values. 3. Digital media—Social aspects.
4. Computer games—Design. I. Nissenbaum, Helen Fay. II. Title.
GV1469.17.S63F63   2014
794.8—dc23
2013043220

10 9 8 7 6 5 4 3 2 1

Contents

9   Reflections on Values at Play   163

Acknowledgments

This book and Values at Play reflect many years of research and exploration—from the start of the Values at Play project in 2005 to the final stroke of editing. Never alone in these endeavors, we benefitted from the support, brilliance, intellectual generosity, and attention of others. As ideas unfolded, we were afforded invaluable opportunities to try them out with audiences of scholars and researchers, with expert gamers as well as the newly initiated, with accomplished designers as well as the eager novice. Our ideas were shaped by their insights, comments, and criticisms, often in ways that are impossible to discern but, here, we wish to acknowledge.

For material and financial support we are grateful for a grant from the National Science Foundation's Science of Design program for our collaborative project: Values at Play—Integrating Social Factors into Design (CNS 0613893), awarded September 2006. Other NSF grants that supported crucial aspects of the Values at Play model include the Cyber-Trust (CT) Collaborative award: CT-M: Privacy, Compliance and Information Risk in Complex Organizational Processes (CNS-0831124), and an EAGER award: Values in Design in the Future Internet Architecture (CNS/NetS 1058333). The bias games discussed in chapter 5 emerged from an EAGER award, Transforming STEM for Women and Girls: Reworking Stereotypes and Bias (HRD-1137483), awarded September 2011. The Intel Science and Technology Center for Social Computing has provided a fertile environment as well as financial support enabling the writing and completion of the manuscript. A grant from the Lady Davis Fellowship Trust, supported a sabbatical semester as a Visiting Professor at the Hebrew University of Jerusalem, Department of Communication and Journalism, and allowed uninterrupted time to work on the manuscript. Mary Flanagan is grateful for Dartmouth College support in her role as the Sherman Fairchild–named chair.

Conferences and universities where we've grown games with *Grow-a-Game* include: Games for Change NYC; Different Games; IndieCade;

Technology for Peace; Playing for Change UK; Grassroots Media Conference; the Game Developers Conference; Games, Learning, and Society; the Digital Games Research Association; the Virtual 2006 conference; and the ACM CHI conference. We gratefully acknowledge audience comments at the University of Pennsylvania's Annenberg School for Communication Colloquium, the Digital Humanities Center and Department of Philosophy Colloquium at Dartmouth University, the University of Illinois at Urbana-Champaign's, Information Trust Institute Lecture, the International Conference of Computer Ethics at Ionian University, Corfu, Greece, the Information Science Program Colloquium at Cornell University, a lecture hosted by the Humanities Center at Carnegie-Mellon University, and a lecture at the Center for International Education at University of Wisconsin–Milwaukee, among others. Students in Nissenbaum's Values in Technology classes at NYU (Media, Culture and Communication) have wrestled with iterations of Values at Play and along the way inspired improvements.

The Values in Design Summer PhD workshops held in 2008 at Santa Clara University and in 2010 at New York University, in collaboration with Geof Bowker and the late Susan Leigh Star, were exciting venues for presenting Values at Play. Participants wholeheartedly engaged with theory and methodology, contributed GAG card games and ideas that have influenced our thinking to this day.

The book owes an enormous debt to past collaborative and coauthored works, most significantly, those with Daniel Howe, Jonathan Belman, and James Diamond, which contributed to the formation of both the theory and structure of Values at Play as well as its pedagogical and design applications. Jonathan Belman was a contributor on chapter 3 in this book and helped dig up examples throughout. Christopher Egert was author of the original *Grow-a-Game* digital deck, and Jack Boffa programmed *Grow-a-Game* for iPhone.

We offer special thanks to the amazing VAP Advisory Board: Katie Salen, Frank Lantz, Tracy Fullerton, Celia Pearce, Jesper Juul. Many exciting conversations, including challenging and supportive insights, inspired us and shaped our work. Several of these advisors wrote short sections in the book, and in addition we welcome the work of Karen Schrier and Kyle Rentschler.

For outstanding research and editorial work, thanks to Emily Goldsher-Diamond, Kyle Rentschler, Toni Pizza, and Mark Essig. Their superhuman efforts at every stage of the book propelled us forward and kept us going. To our rock-star acquisitions editor, Doug Sery, thanks for your faith and enthusiasm. To anonymous reviewers of the final draft, to Deborah

Cantor-Adams of the editorial staff, and to the production staff at the MIT Press, we are deeply grateful for helping us to produce a better book.

Gratitude to key members of our research teams: Sukdith Punjasthitkul, Max Seidman, Anna Lotko, Zara Downs, Suyin Looui, James Bachhuber, John Fanning, Brian Mayzak, Greg Kohl, Jarah Moesch, Jennifer Jacobs, Vanessa Moy, Geoff Kaufman, Danielle Taylor, Grace Peng, Paul Orbell, Chris Takeuchi, Brendan Scully.

Friends, colleagues, comrades, and supporters: Jeff Watson, Naomi Clark, Drew Davidson, Doris Rusch, JoEllen Fisherkeller, Brian Myzak, Angela Ferraiolo, Jose Zagal, Lindsay Gupton, Katherine Isbister, Suzanne Seggerman, Ben Stokes, Suzanna Ruiz, Alice Bonvicini, Zsuzanna Mitro, and the fine folks at Furtherfield.

Thanks for ongoing inspiration from the VID community, and in particular Geof Bowker, Paul Dourish, Batya Friedman, Cory Knobel, Phoebe Sengers, and Michael Zimmer.

Important thanks go to the designers who shared their powerful stories with us for this book.

We are grateful to several organizations for using our methods and contributing to their iterative improvement: Mouse, WQED, Design Studio for Social Intervention Youth Activism Design Institute (YADI), RMIT's GEElab, and the Salzburg Global Seminars.

The significant people in our lives—friends and family—support, nourish, and balance us in indescribable but essential ways. This book is a tribute to them.

MF: I dedicate this book to my family, avid game players one and all, and in particular to my mother, Rose Flanagan, who encouraged early entry to worlds of play.

HN: To my dear family Peter, Dana, Zoe, and Ann Sarnak, thank you for keeping me focused on important things. I dedicate this book to my mother, Rose Nissenbaum, who passed away in August 2013. She was a consummate player of games—a fierce yet fair competitor.

Introducing Values at Play

In 2007, the video game developer BioWare released *Mass Effect*, a role-playing game that contains short flashes of sexual activity toward the end of the game. The game allows players to watch the sex but not to play through the sex, and the scenes are less explicit than many that can be found on network television shows. The relationships between the characters develop over time, there is no complete frontal nudity, and the sex scenes occupy around two minutes of a thirty-hour experience.

The designers of the game were proud of its innovative relationship design and its mix of male, female, and androgynous characters. Players choose to play either male or female forms of the character Shepard, and both versions are equally capable fighters. Intimate relationships are a subplot in the game and are a result of a long chain of conversations and action-fueled missions. *Mass Effect* offers players an opportunity to participate in a complex saga and engage with political and humanitarian issues.

A Fox News Channel television show called *The Live Desk* nonetheless devoted a long segment to the game in early 2008, spurred on by blogger Kevin McCullough, who stated that *Mass Effect* players could "engage in the most realistic sex acts ever conceived" and "hump in every form, format, multiple, gender-oriented possibility they can think of."[1] A member of the panel discussion described it as "Luke Skywalker meets *Debbie Does Dallas*." Panelists claimed that the game featured on-demand graphic sex, and a psychological specialist asserted that playing *Mass Effect* could pervert the psychosexual development of young boys.[2]

These reactions are not unusual. Games are subject to far more scrutiny than network television or Hollywood films and often are condemned by people who do not play them. Most critics adopt a so-called family values stance, and their critiques tend to be either misinformed or intentionally misleading. The claims of psychological damage to youth, such as those made on *Fox News*, are unfounded.[3] But such statements help to shape the common misperception that all video games belong to a hyperviolent, hypersexualized wasteland. No wonder game designers and players get nervous whenever the words *games* and *values* are mentioned in the same breath. Game makers, justifiably soured on the topic, often simply refuse to engage in a discussion about the relationship between games and values.

This is understandable but also unfortunate. As a medium for learning, entertainment, and communication, games are an increasingly prominent part of the current cultural landscape. Ignoring values in games may seem the best way to answer provocations like those of the Fox News panel, but it also means missing important opportunities to diversify the field and promote innovation.

The team behind this book—at Dartmouth College (the Tiltfactor Laboratory) and at New York University—has been studying the territory of human values and games for almost a decade. We call our research Values at Play because we are committed to nurturing a constructive discourse about games and values. Unlike many politicians and pundits who invoke values to advocate censorship or scold designers for controversial content, we approach this topic critically, not moralistically. We're interested in the role that values play in animating personal, political, and artistic expression through any medium. We aim to provide resources for designers and design students who are interested in exploring the creative potential of what we call values-conscious design and who wish to consider, in a systematic way, the moral, social, and political resonances of digital games.

Our work coalesces the activities of making games, playing games, thinking about games, and theorizing about the relationship between digital technologies and values. As both theorists and practitioners, we have discovered that any ideas applied to games must account for the distinguishing properties of the medium, such as its rule-based architecture, player agency, interactivity, and the nature of gaming as a cultural phenomenon. When it comes to ethical and political values in games, this challenge is no different. We have developed game-specific modes of analysis and design methodologies and created actual games manifesting values-conscious design. The methodology that we have developed is complementary to standard design practices in a practical way.

The project has three core premises—that societies have common (not necessarily universal) values; that technologies, including digital games, embody ethical and political values; and that those who design digital games have the power to shape players' engagement with these values. We have coined the term *conscientious designer* to describe those who accept these premises and commit to considering values when they design and

Figure 0.1
Commander Shepard and Liara T'Soni embracing, from the video game *Mass Effect* (2007).

build systems. When our book speaks to the design community, it is less to persuade skeptics to accept these three premises than to invite those who take values seriously—the conscientious designer—to try out Values at Play.

This book includes a theoretical and practical introduction to Values at Play. Part I introduces Values at Play. Chapter 1 introduces core themes that contribute to the book's theoretical grounding, explaining the theory of values adopted in this book and the reasons that values should be a core consideration in game design. Chapter 2 includes deep readings of a handful of games to demonstrate the diverse ways in which values are embedded in all games. Chapter 3 provides a systemic way to look at values and identifies fifteen game elements (including the narrative structure of the game, the game engine that it uses, and the context in which a player encounters it) that together form a game's semantic architecture, through which its values are conveyed.

Part II examines the Values at Play heuristic. In chapter 4, we introduce the Values at Play heuristic, which is a practical guide for conscientious designers that offers a way to incorporate values into the iterative design process. The methodology has three stages—discovering values related to and embedded within a given game project (chapter 5), implementing those values in design features and game elements (chapter 6), and verifying that the desired values actually appear in the game (chapter 7).

Finally, part III discusses Values at Play at work. In chapter 8, we examine how this methodology can inspire designers, especially through tools that we have developed (such as the Values at Play curriculum and Grow-a-Game cards). Parts II and III include short essays by game designers and thinkers. Their first-person accounts explain how they have put thinking about values and the Values at Play theory into practice—with notable success. Throughout the book and especially in the conclusion (chapter 9), we argue that consideration of values should be integral, not incidental, to the design of all games. Putting values at play helps designers create games that are more fun, more innovative, and more deeply engaged with the world in which we live.

I   Understanding Values at Play

1 Groundwork for Values in Games

All games express and embody human values. From notions of fairness to deep-seated ideas about the human condition, games provide a compelling arena where humans play out their beliefs and ideas. To anthropologists, games are paradigmatic among human practices and rituals. From the misty origins of the classic Go game in Asia to the more recent evolution of chess and online games such as *World of Warcraft* (Blizzard Entertainment 2004), games can serve as cultural snapshots: they capture beliefs from a particular time and place and offer ways to understand what a given group of people believes and values. These beliefs may be made visible on the surface (through game characters or other visual features), and they may be expressed through a game's many elements (such as point of view, actions, and hardware). A player's available choices can express a particular understanding of the world, such as the extent to which fate either is in the hands of individuals or societies or is subject to the uncontrollable forces of nature and serendipity. Many elements of games reveal the underlying beliefs and values of their designers and players. Further, because games are engrossing and reach deep parts of the human psyche, they may not only reflect and express but also activate these beliefs and values in powerful ways.

We propose three key reasons why it's important to study values in games. First, the study of games enriches our understanding of how deep-seated sociocultural patterns are reflected in norms of participation, play, and communication. Second, the growth in digital media and expanding cultural significance of games constitutes both an opportunity and responsibility for the design community to reflect on the values that are expressed in games. Third, games have emerged as the media paradigm of the twenty-first century, surpassing film and television in popularity; they have the power to shape work, learning, health care, and more.

Why are there so many games being produced and sold *right now*? Technology has advanced to the point where digital games can flourish in myriad forms and give players true agency in complex digital playspaces. The large number of games emerging from independent makers and big game design companies demonstrates that there is room for new kinds of game experiences to be created and to find audiences. We pay attention to games because we are players and designers and also because games tell stories and allow players to engage with systems that help them understand the complexities of contemporary life.

Why Games Are Different

Games have become a central way that we tell stories embedded in larger systems of belief and interaction across cultures, and their recurring conventions, themes, player rituals and actions, and music may function as a means of mythmaking. Theories borrowed from literature, television, and film studies do not fully address the psychological, social, and mythic power of games. The emerging generation of game theorists recognizes the role that digital games play as a distinctive cultural artifact and have begun to theorize about player agency, identity, and rules within a community of play.[1]

We do not wish to overstate individual player agency. Neither do we wish to understate the debt that digital games owe to the vast contemporary cultural landscape, including science and other art forms. The interactive and iterative nature of digital media is similar to that of analog games, choose-your-own adventure books, and participatory television (such as *American Idol*).[2] Contemporary computer games offer a range of interactive experiences, from predetermined choose-your-own-adventure stories like *Fable* (Lionhead Studios 2004) to dynamic, unpredictable systems that use physics models, multiplayer interaction, and emergence, such as *World of Goo* (2D Boy 2008) or *Minecraft* (Mojang 2011).

The distinctive effect that games have also may be due to their immersive character: players actively control and identify with playable characters, and their actions typically shape situations within the game experience.[3] Whether or not experiences of agency within games transfer out into real-world contexts, at the very least such agency distinguishes the experience of game playing from film or television viewing. Beyond role playing and perspective taking, digital games offer players a dynamic engagement with content through cycles of effort, attention, and feedback. Unlike traditional forms of other media, which do not respond to players' journeys or to their readings and interpretations, digital games are particularly compelling environments in which players explore and act based on at least a partial understanding of a system's relational dynamics. As Janet Murray has observed, games give us "a chance to enact our most basic relationship to the world—our desire to prevail over adversity, to survive our inevitable defeats, to shape our environment, to master complexity, and to make our lives fit together like the pieces of a jigsaw puzzle."[4] Beyond merely telling stories as traditional narratives do, digital games allow for enactment and provide a systems-level rule set for the story's logic.

What Values? Whose Values?

When we discuss Values at Play, people often ask, "What values? Whose values? And what are values, anyway?" These are entirely reasonable questions given the many meanings of *values* and *value* as they are used both colloquially and in academic scholarship. Values also provoke controversy within and across societies, among individuals, and even within a single person. As Isaiah Berlin notes, "Values may easily clash within the breast of a single individual; and it does not follow that, if they do, some must be true and others false."[5] Full answers to these general questions lie beyond the scope of this book, but enough must be said about values to convey the basic terms of our theory of Values at Play.

Simply put, values are properties of things and states of affairs that we care about and strive to attain. They are similar to goals, purposes, and ends, but usually they possess a higher degree of gravitas and permanence, and they tend to be more abstract and general. Thus, while you might set a goal to exercise and lose three pounds, it would be odd to cite this as a *value*. Instead, the relevant value might be good health. As a value, however, good health takes on a general importance—that is, if I cite good health as one of my values, then I care about good health for not only for myself but also about good health for others. Values may take a variety of forms—qualities of the environment (such as species diversity), personal traits (such as honesty), and political states (such as justice and democracy). Values may be specific to individuals or shared by groups, and they may bind communities, cultures, religions, or nations. We acknowledge these differences by speaking of personal values, cultural values, religious values, human values, and so forth. We may further differentiate among types of values by talking of ethical, political, and aesthetic values and more. Finally, values are often ideals: we promote them even as we accept that we may never achieve them. World peace, tolerance, kindness, and justice are instances of such ideals.

People express their value commitments in a variety of ways. Some reduce values to an economic proposition: how much are people willing to pay to save a species from extinction, promote the health of a population, or ensure territorial security? Although this approach may be useful for practical public policy decisions,[6] we adopt a more pluralistic approach. In addition to expressing their commitments through economic decisions, people also express them through symbolic gestures, artworks, words, companions, work, and—as we assert throughout this book—their designs for things they build.

Although the range of values is virtually boundless, here we are interested primarily in ethical and political values. Typical examples of ethical values include kindness, honesty, generosity, fidelity, integrity, respect, safety, autonomy, creativity, peace, pleasure, well-being, friendship, collaboration, health, responsibility, happiness, and contentment. All of these contribute to the moral dimension of our lives—how we treat others and how they treat us. Political values include those that define relationships within and between societies, such as justice, equality, security, stability, cooperation, tolerance, privacy, accountability, democracy, voice, property, liberty, liberation, autonomy, equal opportunity, and government transparency. As the scholar Langdon Winner notes, political values are "arrangements of power and authority."[7]

Narrowing our attention to ethically and politically significant values still leaves plenty of room for controversy over what values and whose values count. Noting differences in values between people and societies, some have asked, "My personal values may be different from yours, and our societal, religious, and cultural values may be different. How can you presume to select particular values and particular versions of those values?"

Such questions emerged in Western philosophical traditions as far back as the ancient Greeks, and to this day they continue to play important roles in debates over the existence of basic human values, moral and cultural relativism, the politics of recognition,[8] and critical theory. Plato considered goodness, justice, and beauty to be objective, universal human values. In contrast, the twentieth-century anthropologist Ruth Benedict argues, on the basis of her ethnographic research, that values in human societies are infinitely elastic and that none rises to the status of universal.[9] Benjamin Franklin's list of eleven values to guide his life include cleanliness, frugality, industry, moderation, silence, temperance, and sincerity. But why single out these, and should Franklin's values serve as a guide for others? Social psychologists have conducted research to try to discover which values might be universal across diverse nations and cultures. Milton Rokeach suggests a core of common values, which he divides into two categories—terminal values (such as a comfortable life and freedom) and instrumental values (such as honesty and cooperation).[10] Although doubts persist about the list's comprehensiveness, there has been general scholarly agreement that the values "cover a broad spectrum."[11] Shalom Schwartz and Wolfgang Bilsky posit three classes of universal values that are based on three distinct needs—biological needs, interactional needs for interpersonal coordination, and societal needs serving group survival and welfare.[12]

Although these theories of universal human values drawn from biological, individual, and social needs are of compelling interest, a theory of Values at Play does not depend on them. Our approach does not require universal values, but it does presume the existence of socially recognized moral and political values—that is, the positive ends that a society strives to enshrine in its institutional, political, and social structures and that it encourages individuals to adopt as a guide. Political philosophers, ethicists, religious and secular leaders, teachers, parents, and peers all engage in the study, deliberation, definition, propagation, and communication of these values, sometimes explicitly in words and decrees and other times through actions and reactions. Although deploying the theory presumes a stance on values, it does not presume any particular stance, instead allowing for divergence of worldviews. One system of values might emphasize freedom, and another might favor responsibility, but both provide a sound platform for the Values at Play model.

Here is the stance that we have adopted throughout the book: as citizens of a liberal, egalitarian democracy, we hold a bias in favor of values such as respect for human rights, the rule of law, individual freedom, justice, and the basic equality of all human beings. We are inspired by foundational political documents, including the U.S. Constitution, the Charter of the United Nations, and the Canadian Charter of Rights and Freedoms. We also depend on literatures in ethics and political philosophy as well as ideals embodied in religious documents. From the high-minded to the vernacular, these sources reveal a resilient core. Values that we encounter in these explorations include justice, equality, freedom, autonomy, security, happiness, privacy, tolerance, cooperation, creativity, generosity, trust, equity, diversity, fidelity, integrity, environmentalism, liberation, self-determination, democracy, and tradition. These commonly encountered, socially recognized values are points of departure for Values at Play.

We are aware that there are differences in values across societies and individuals. Gender equity, for example, is explicitly recognized in the United States but not in Saudi Arabia. With even the most commonly encountered values, differences emerge in the ways that they are interpreted and applied. Plato, for example, favors equality in general but not for slaves or women. A theory of Values at Play is not going to resolve issues that have united and divided people and societies for centuries. There is little choice but to take a stand where a stand is needed. Those who build social institutions and who institute social practices make these determinations all the time: we pass laws, strike treaties, and develop educational systems. We return to our thinkers and writers, and we turn to the people who are served by—or must suffer under—these systems and institutions. These people, in turn, express their values in the ways that they vote, respond to surveys, and make financial and commercial choices.

Values in Technology

Values at Play adds one further dimension to the values landscape. It asserts that digital games—like other technologies and like social practices, systems, and institutions—have values embedded in them. In so saying, we place ourselves within the larger discussion about values in technology. As Langdon Winner argues in his landmark article "Do Artifacts Have Politics?," the creators of technical systems and devices should consider functional and material properties and also recognize the ethical and political properties of these technologies. The crucial insight of Winner's article, which has been refined and elaborated many different ways by the author and others,[13] is that the values expressed in technical systems are a function of their uses as well as their features and design.[14] Privacy is one such value. For example, early versions of the Unix operating system that include the "finger" command to ascertain if a colleague was online might be judged hostile to privacy, and a discussion board that allows anonymous posts might be deemed privacy friendly (more such examples are woven throughout this book). In such ways, we might consider privacy or other values to be embedded in the design of the technology. But reading values into and out of technical systems is not simple as even our two quick examples reveal. "Finger" may seem intrusive to present day users of the Internet but in the early days of Unix, the users of a given system would more than likely be colleagues, even friends or members of a common community and the "finger" command more likely the inquiry of colleague to colleague rather than a problematic intrusion. The expansion to a global environment that many digital systems have attained—both large-scale systems (such as the Internet) and relatively modest sized ones (such as games themselves)—this embedding of values further complicates pressing issues worthy of our attention.

The notion that values are embedded in technology motivates a practical turn in the work on values in design. We can do more than simply demonstrate systematic relationships between technology and values; we can do something about it. If we accept that technology can embody values, the practical turn allows designers and producers to consider ethical and political concerns alongside more typical engineering ideals. System design is typically guided by goals such as reliability, efficiency, resilience, modularity, performance, safety, and cost. We suggest adding items like fairness, equality, and sustainability to the list. Because conscientious designers have the opportunity to integrate values into their everyday practice, they can have a hand in determining which values are expressed.

The idea that values should be considered in the design of technical systems has spurred initiatives such as values-conscious design and values-sensitive design.[15] Values at Play offers an alternative approach for guiding technical design for digital games, which are challenging because of their hybridity: they are games, expressive art forms, and technological engines. The first two aspects—game and art form—are generally visible to users as well as critics and theorists. They include storylines, plots, settings, narratives, characters, colors, shapes, landscapes, sound, music, and interface as well as game goals, rules, challenges, representational systems, competitive constructs, and reward systems. These elements have garnered most of the attention in discussions of the social significance of digital games. This is partly because such elements are immediately experienced and therefore obvious but also because highly developed, time-honored theoretical frameworks—borrowed from media, art, sound, cinema, and literary criticism—are able to address them. In other words, there is a rich vocabulary for exploring the plot, character, and rules of digital games.

The same cannot be said for the technological architecture of games. Scholars of values in technology still push against the received view of technology as neutral, and even though this area of study remains active, controversial, and unsettled, it provokes questions and generates approaches that are explored in this book.[16] Yet just as narrative and game rules carry values, so do lines of code, game engines, mechanics, and hardware. The Values at Play approach is interested in all three of the hybrid layers—expressive, ludic, and technological. Our aim is to contribute to a critical language for technology that is as rich as those that exist for expressive art.[17]

Values at and in Play

It is impossible to do justice to the range and depth of inquiry into values in technology, design, and games in the few paragraphs that we have devoted to these topics in this chapter. We aim primarily to give a sense of the rich heritage that inspires our decidedly pragmatic focus. With concrete cases throughout the book, the text illustrates systematic relationships between values and particular design elements. (Readers interested in plumbing greater depths may find further direction in our bibliographic references.) For example, the bestselling PC game of all time, *The Sims* (Maxis 2000), has been said to inculcate materialist values that define the home as a space that primarily is devoted to consumption. Players are encouraged to earn money and spend it on acquiring goods, especially household goods (such as furniture and televisions) and eventually larger homes.[18] *Saints Row* (Volition, Inc. 2006) is a game series in which crime pays. It portrays the world as a violent place that rewards criminal behavior (such as insurance fraud) and reinforces racial and gender stereotypes. The "Whored" mode in *Saints Row: The Third* (Volition, Inc. 2011) features waves of attacking prostitutes, and "The Penetrator" weapon (a deadly purple dildo baseball bat) is used against them.[19] In a gentler vein, the player in *Okami* (Clover Studio 2006) takes on the role of the animal/goddess Amaterasu, whose job is to make plants and animals happy in the environment. We may say that this game fosters empathy, nurturing, sharing, and care-giving.

Claims such as these, however, deserve close scrutiny if we wish to avoid a similar, simplistic determinism that would have bound the "finger" command to a violation of privacy. The tongue-in-cheek tone of *The Sims*, for example, and its presentation of consumerism as monotonous resist facile interpretations and evoke more complicated responses from players. Although our perspective supports the need for this more nuanced interpretation of values in games, we recognize that there are no simple lines that connect characteristics of a game's elements (such as content, architecture, and actions) with the attainment (or suppression) of certain values and valued states. Just as the connection between "finger" and privacy required an understanding of subtle dynamics introduced by shifting contexts of use, so the features of a game as bearers of values emerge in the act of play, dynamically, depending on the context of play and who is playing. Designers' intentions matter but are not fully determinative; unintended values may be served in spite of these intentions, and intended values may fall flat.[20]

Inspired by games, we chose the phrase *Values at Play* as the label for our framework to acknowledge the multidimensional flux of these complexities in the design domain. The term *play* has many meanings, including "perform a role"; "occupy oneself in amusement, sport, or fantasy"; "play along with and accept the rules in a given situation"; and "allow a space for movement, as in the free play of gears." Values at Play shares roots with recent important work in ethics in games, focusing on ethical choices and the ways that ethical and unethical actions are structured within games. Values at Play incorporates a perspective on ethical actions, valued ends, and direct and indirect ways that game elements involve values.[21] Recognizing these important shared roots, we have included a short contribution by Karen Schrier, one of the leading contributors to the study of ethics in games.

Yet complexity does not mean anarchy. Admitting that the interdependencies along the pathway from design to values (and back again) are complex and diverse does not warrant nihilism and resignation any more here than in the myriad other circumstances in which thoughtful action is required despite uncertainties. Questioning one's own worldview is a good start. A conscientious designer might proceed by holding fixed certain variables while manipulating others, learning about who is likely to play (and their worldviews), and exploring the likely context of play. These considerations are all part of the toolkit of a designer who is aiming for a holistic approach to making design choices with values in mind. Although the philosophical rubrics associated with values in technology and values in design are the context for this book, the concrete and the nitty-gritty are our dominant vernacular. We examine the ways that values have been and may be enacted, denied, confronted, and manipulated—the ways that values are "at play" in games and design.

Introducing the Conscientious Designer

These are our core premises: (1) there are common (not necessarily universal) values; (2) artifacts may embody ethical and political values; and (3) steps taken in design and development have the power to affect the nature of these values.

Professionals may discover core values while they are working in their respective fields. Donald Schön has related this type of discovery to notions of reflective practice. His work helped us forge thinking about design professions and brought to light ways that design practitioners might be more reflective or, in our terms, conscientious.[22] His foundational work takes on the challenges of problem setting (asking the right question) over problem solving, noting that many professionals learn about these challenges the hard way by asking the wrong question and trying to solve for the wrong goal. If problems are not well defined initially, then poor results emerge. This thinking is relevant to game design processes, especially when designers think that they are instilling one set of values but actually may be embedding another.

Our goal is to help designers seek an active role in shaping the social, ethical, and political values that may be embedded in games. When those values inevitably veer off course during the process of iteration, designers need to be confident enough to bring them back on track even when it is difficult to do so.

Conscientious designers consider values when they design and build systems. They often have a passion for learning, a deep curiosity about the world, and a fascination with human behavior. This passion is expressed in well-thought-through design. Our book does not try to persuade skeptics in the design community to accept these premises but instead invites conscientious designers to try the Values at Play heuristic. If you are interested in taking values seriously in design, you are a conscientious designer. To you, we offer Values at Play.

This book is intended as a resource that is grounded in theory but essentially practical. Values at Play is a theory insofar as it constitutes a structured way to understand values in games. As a theoretical framework, it provides a lens through which designers can appreciate values in a game, just as other theoretical approaches guide people to appreciate other dimensions, such as aesthetics, technological efficacy, or narrative. But the purpose of Values at Play is primarily pragmatic. It is a companion for designers who seek to make new and better games by considering values, who accept relationships between design and values, and who ask how we might convert these insights into practices in the world.

Innumerable decisions fall within the scope of our project, because values may be at play at all levels of a design initiative. From overarching architectural principles to decisions at the finest grain, designers and software engineers can influence the shape of an initiative through choices and problem-solving strategies. Although our book reveals philosophical implications of human values that are at play in digital games, its central claims are asserted in terms of concrete examples—many of them—demonstrating connections between abstract ideas about values and games to moment-by-moment decisions in the design process.

Drawing on theory-based principles and practical insights from scholarship and design practice, this book develops a method for integrating values in the conception and design of games that can serve as a guide for games designers and developers. Conscientious designers are ethical (they are truthful, factual, and alert and have the player's best interests at heart) and also strive to make a difference through their work. The number of conscientious designers is steadily increasing, and as they work, they will find that values appear in a range of games and their constitutive elements. It is essential to identify the issues and address those moment-to-moment decisions about values in game development. The conscientious designer needs backup—prior evidence, support materials, and methods—and we provide such backup in this book.

In the relatively short history of information technologies, stories of its moral and political significance abound in the informal lore and in carefully researched cases. They discuss the Internet's democratizing potential, the Web's free and equitable access to knowledge, the diminishing privacy brought about by databases and cookies, and so on. Such stories raise questions about whether these social and political outcomes are accidental or whether they can be integrated into the day-to-day goals and practices of technology design, thereby giving rise to better technologies. Can conscientious designers change society for the better with their work? Our commitment to positive answers to these questions motivates the Values at Play project. Although our ideals are tempered with a good dose of realism, we continue to work toward change by putting social and political values on the design agenda so that it can lead to better games and better technology.

2 Uncovering Values at Play

The twentieth-century media scholar Marshall McLuhan—who coined the expression "the medium is the message"—once argued that "all media exist to invest our lives with artificial perceptions and arbitrary values."[1] The goal of Values at Play is to make the values in one medium—digital games—slightly less arbitrary. Before designers can take control of the values in their games, however, they must analyze and discover exactly where values crop up in the first place. In this chapter, we analyze existing games from a values perspective.

Every game expresses a set of values, but it's often difficult to understand the many ways in which those values come to be embodied in the game. To untangle these many factors, it's useful to group them into two broad categories—designer understandings and player perceptions. Designer understandings encompass the broad range of values that emerge in the creation of a game. The company or organization that is building the game faces economic and commercial constraints, creates business and marketing plans, and makes educated guesses about consumers' preferences, and each of these actions brings values into play. Public policy, industry regulations that govern games, and the general cultures in which the games are created also play roles. Values emerge in the definition of a project and in the specifications of instrumental design features. Designers bring preexisting value commitments to their work and make assumptions about the values of their target audiences. Finally, the expectations of various stakeholders (investors, executives, and more) also shape a game's values.

And the story is far from over when the game is created and released because player perceptions also contribute to a game's values. People playing the same game may not have identical values experiences because personal, cultural, and situational factors all influence players' experience of values in a game each time they play the same game.

Uncovering Values in Nondigital Games

For some people, American football promotes values of violence, antagonism, and territoriality. Others, however, see cooperation and teamwork at the game's core. Both interpretations can be rooted in people's real experiences of the game, and these views should not necessarily be understood as conflicting with each other. A person might view football in both ways at once—that is, she could experience "the values of football" as a complex interrelationship of violence, antagonism, territoriality, cooperation, and teamwork.[2] All of these values emerge from the rules of the game, and any combination of them might contribute to a player's experience of the game's values. Precisely how players or spectators experience the values of football depends on the unique combination of personal, cultural, and situational factors that they bring to the game.

Player perceptions, of course, do not operate in a vacuum. Game mechanics and narrative elements create constraints that preclude some interpretations and steer players toward others. It would be difficult, for example, to interpret football as an affirmation of nonviolence. Since violence is clearly sanctioned by the rules (that is, it's OK to tackle other players), such an interpretation would be implausible. Likewise, it would be difficult for players to experience football as an affirmation or a violation of the value of privacy because privacy is simply not a focus of the game. The point is, we can rule out or minimize some interpretations while also describing a range of plausible and relevant interpretations.

The goal of Values at Play is to draw attention to that range of plausible interpretations and to ensure that the values embedded in games are not "arbitrary" (to use McLuhan's term) but rather a matter for careful consideration. For conscientious designers, a game's values are a core focus of the design of the game, because they understand that each of the myriad decisions that go into the design of a game create constraints that define the range of plausible interpretations within a game.

A good way to shed light on these issues is to take an already existing game, add or subtract a mechanic or key game feature, and investigate how such modifications change the range of plausible interpretations. Consider an alteration to the rules of American football in which players begin the game with their jersey numbers obscured by a patch, and any player whose number is still obscured cannot be called for penalties. In addition to running, passing, and tackling, players on both sides also would attempt to tear away the patches on their opponents' jerseys. Players with concealed numbers might resort to underhanded or even dangerous plays because the rule would allow them to do so.

This one rule change has a ripple effect, altering the experience of playing the game; it also changes the range of possible value interpretations. Under the new rules, the values of privacy and secrecy are "activated" and brought to the forefront. These values are minor features of football under its standard rules, where huddles remain private, and communication between players and coaches is often conducted in a secret language of hand signals and coded play calls. Under the new rules, however, privacy and secrecy become key elements of the game and govern how players interact. In the game as normally played, we wouldn't expect every player to experience privacy, but under the new rules, privacy is a value that is very much at play.

Now consider another non-digital game: an ancient game called mancala that can be traced back to some of the world's earliest civilizations. A group of games known as the mancala family of games emerged in northern Africa as early as 6900 BC;[3] ancient mancala boards made with cupping marks (depressions in the earth or a stone) have been discovered at both ordinary and grand archeological sites. The game involves distributing, capturing, and redistributing tokens (beads, stones, or seeds) on a game board with two to four rows of indentions. A player removes all the stones from a cup and distributes them one by one into the other cups across the board, with the goal of capturing the stones from the board (figure 2.1). The rules

Figure 2.1
Children playing mancala.

vary considerably across various versions, but in all of them, the process of playing is much like sowing seeds in a field. In some societies today, the game remains a popular pastime that also happens to be relevant to a dominant economic activity, farming.

What values are at play in such an ancient, seemingly simple game? Game play in mancala is usually symmetric, meaning that players use the same strategy, identical resources, and the same rules. Also apparent is the quality of perfect information. All information is available to all players: all the pieces are available to players at the start of the game, and there are no hidden elements or rules. No player holds any particular advantage, and therefore anyone can possibly win the game. We could therefore say that the game embodies the values of fairness and equality. As in nearly all games, a player needs to trust that the opposing player will play by the rules and not, for example, slip a stone into the wrong bin in violation of the rules. Because mancala focuses on the act of distributing and gathering, it engages, by way of a harvesting metaphor, the notions of nature and sustenance. For many groups, the game represents a cultural tradition that can be shared with another player of similar background or taught to an outsider. When it is played in public, a game may also foster community. So playing a casual game of mancala might engage the values of fairness, equality, trust, nature, sustenance, tradition, and community. It is worth noting that values such as tradition and community are not enshrined in the game's rules. Instead, they are embedded in the materials used in the boards, the presentation of the game, and the context created by the community where it is played.

Now, consider how mancala could be modified to introduce new values. Certain stones, for example, could take on special powers that allow a player to clear an entire spot on the opponent's side of the board, which would play on the tension between competition and cooperation. Or if the stones in a cup appeared in a particular color combination (such as all blue), that collection could be removed from the board and distributed between the players, introducing the value of sharing.

Through these examples, we've seen that values crop up across game formats and types, regardless of technology. Although digital games may afford certain values over others, physical games, such as football and mancala, demonstrate that digital media are not unique in allowing values to be manipulated through design choices. When game designers recognize how a small rule change or representation can affect values, they can weave particular values into the fabric of a game.

Uncovering Values in Digital Games

Any game can be unpacked for its values. Using the same critical tools that we used with football and mancala, we can discover values in digital games and examine how these values are revealed and enacted through play.

Ico

Ico (Sony Computer Entertainment 2001) is an award-winning game from the first years of the release of Sony's PlayStation 2 video game console. In *Ico*, the player takes on the role of the title character in a dark, fictionalized world. Ico is an ostracized boy who is abandoned in an isolated castle as a village sacrifice. In the castle, he encounters a girl named Yorda, a bright, shimmering teenager who also finds herself locked in the castle (figure 2.2). The player's goal in controlling Ico is to keep Yorda safe from the demons that pursue her and to help her escape the treacherous location, which is surrounded by dangerous cliffs and crevasses. The black spirits attempt to drag Yorda down into their portals, and battles ensue. Although Yorda is less agile than Ico, she can perform certain tasks in the castle (such as open idol doors) that Ico cannot. Yorda seldom speaks, but when she does, the player cannot understand her language. Fumito Ueda, a game designer for Sony, reveals himself to be a conscientious designer when he posed this question in his keynote address at the 2002 Game Developers Conference: "What kind of 'reality' can generate emotional involvement, or 'empathy'"?[4] Ueda takes up this challenge, creating a reality in which empathy lies front and center.

Figure 2.2
Yorda and Ico, from *Ico* (Sony Computer Entertainment 2001).

Ueda's vision for the game was fulfilled. On blogs, game reviews, and game-play walkthroughs, many players have described their experiences with *Ico* as deeply moving. The game's narrative fosters strong empathy for Yorda, and the same value is built into the game's mechanics, so that the game player's actions foster empathy.[5] The environment of the castle heightens the emotion. The haunting environmental audio design features the crash of waves on the cliffs below, footsteps that echo cavernously in the castle, gulls that cry, and gears that groan as doors move. This sonic environment evokes loneliness and fear.[6] Because Yorda is not as mobile as Ico, players must create safe passage by lowering bridges, climbing ropes, and the like. Often Yorda can do more than she seems to think she can: she can climb ladders and run quickly if Ico encourages her. Ico catches Yorda's hand to help her cross wide gaps, often lifting her to safety. The relationship between the two struggling young people is captured in romantic and touching ways, such as showing them at game-save points holding hands and falling asleep on couches throughout the castle. These in-play depictions, the game's expressive environments, and game mechanics generate a protective, empathetic relationship between the player and Yorda.

Flower

Flower (thatgamecompany 2009) allows players to invade the dreams of urban houseplants, opening up in imaginative space as the flower dream moves into the open plains outside the city (figure 2.3). Players begin the game by playing as the wind, with a single flower petal used to mark the breeze. The petal lets players know which way they are traveling, and it also allows a minimalist approach to the game controls: the player merely tips the game controller one way or the other to guide the petal (and its subsequent chain) through the sky. The player finds that breezing over flowers in the landscape causes them to burst into bloom with a beautiful sound, and each flower that opens also offers one petal to what can become a long kite-tail of flower petals. Players work to help the flowers bloom, gathering petals while moving across the landscape. The action in this level of the game is simple, hypnotic, and beautiful.

Later, however, the game world turns dark. As the player advances through levels, the landscape shifts from vast, healthy fields to postapocalyptic ruins. As the game progresses, a dichotomy emerges between natural elements and human-made objects. Midway through the game, technological objects created by humans begin to appear to be menacing and dangerous. Players who move through these dangerous levels come to understand that antiquated technologies can threaten the flowers that they are helping

Figure 2.3
The beautiful world of *Flower* (thatgamecompany 2009).

to bring to life. The player begins to heal this rift through play, weaving a relationship of balance between vegetation and sustainable technologies, nature and culture. The game retains its state between play times, so players can reenter its realm by simply choosing to begin.

In his 1955 book *Homo Ludens: A Study of the Play-Element in Culture*, the historian Johan Huizinga explains that any type of space that is used for play—whether an arena, a card table, or a screen—creates a "temporary world within the ordinary world, dedicated to the performance of an act apart."[7] Through its load screens, fantasy landscape, music, responsive feedback, and mechanics, *Flower*, like so many other great games, frames a cohesive world apart. *Flower* is an interesting hybrid of an easy-to-play casual game and a console game that requires many hours of dedicated play.

The intuitive, gradually revealed rules of the game (what to collect, what to avoid) reinforce the power of the magic circle. In such exploratory play, players simultaneously submit to and discover the rules that govern the game. As they advance through the levels, they begin to understand that natural elements can be nurtured (producing positive outcomes) or mistreated (leading to destruction). By navigating, players pass repeatedly over land, aim up to the sky to see the length of the "tail" of petals gathered like a kite, and sometimes rush through the grasses to hear and "feel" the grass. There is a nuanced kind of pleasure in exploring the landscape in and of itself, and in experiencing the game's responsive aesthetics. *Flower* favors a contemplative type of play.

The game designer intended this effect. "If you want to touch the player through your game, you have to be successful at letting them *get* some portion of what you are trying to say in the game," Jenova Chen, lead designer for thatgamecompany, has explained. "And if you want the player to really appreciate what you are saying, the message has to be relevant to them. I think it is quite hard today to make a relevant message in video games because the majority of the games happen in a very fake world. It's not just the graphics I'm talking about. I think *feeling* real is very different from *looking* real."[8] If there is realism in *Flower*, it is made manifest partly through the technology of the physics engine and, more importantly, through the path of the wind, which mirrors a kind of thoughtfulness in that the controls create a wide berth for navigation.

How are the values in *Flower* put into play? The interaction of player and game is one of minimal intrusion. Players tilt their game controllers and press only one button to increase the wind velocity. Thus, players have imprecise control in the world. They cannot plant flowers, dig them up, or otherwise manipulate the world in direct ways. Rather, they gently guide or influence the game world. This interaction is a consistent translation of the game's values, which focus on encouraging players to work in partnership with the environment. The meaning in *Flower* is not that wind will fix the world but that working with the whole system is the path to success. "In general, at thatgamecompany, we tend to pick universal themes from everyday life and from the world around us," Chen has noted. "I was lucky to have experienced quite a diversified culture between the West and the East. When I think, I tend to avoid thoughts that are too American or Chinese. I like to feel it from a more open perspective as a genuine human being."[9] Chen's goal—to ground the core ideas and actions of the game in genuine human concerns—reveals the advantages of conscientious design. In this game, the values of balance, sustainability, cooperation, and influence are infused into gameplay.

Beyond Good & Evil

Unlike *Flower*, most video games depict a clear enemy. As its name suggests, the action-adventure game *Beyond Good & Evil* (Ubisoft 2003) brings to the forefront questions of friends and enemies, self and other. Friedrich Nietzsche begins his famous philosophical work *Beyond Good and Evil* (1886) with the question, "SUPPOSING that Truth is a woman—what then?"[10] Nietzsche's statement playfully implies that his fellow philosophers might be vexed by searching for truth in the elusive, mysterious package that a nineteenth-century woman was assumed to be. Readers today might find this suggestion mildly offensive or merely quaint, but game designers at Ubisoft took up the question in their futuristic game. In this game, players act as the character Jade, a female hero who is a martial arts expert. She also is the caretaker of orphans who are animal and human hybrids whose parents were attacked by aliens known as DomZ (figure 2.4). But if truth is a woman (that is, the character Jade), what sort of truth is she?

The game experience is an attractive mix of adventure, action, and puzzle. Living comfortably in a lighthouse on a pretty island on the planet Hillys, the hybrid children and their benefactor come under attack by the DomZ aliens. Unable to pay her electric bill and thus unable to use her home-shield defense, Jade takes a job as a photographer to document the species that have thus far survived the war with the DomZ. Players help Jade document the animals, earn funds, and investigate hidden conspiracies in the war. Unlike most action games, *Beyond Good & Evil* rewards players for evidence that is gathered through photography and not for the number of bodies killed or weapons gathered. The task of documenting species might suggest that the game is supporting the value of biodiversity and warning against mass extinction. This may be true, but it soon becomes clear that something more complicated is at work as well.

As the central role played by the hybrid orphans suggests, the question of natural categories—including racial categories—is central to the game. But are these natural categories posited as good, evil, or somehow beyond? The

Figure 2.4
Jade, from *Beyond Good & Evil* (Ubisoft 2003).

title suggests that the game design transcends this dichotomy, but the game play does not necessarily enable the player to do so. The strange relationship of alien species to Hillys species often leaves the player feeling uneasy about the possibility of transcending a good and evil dichotomy. Jade's job, taking pictures of animals in exchange for credit, exposes the uncertainty of natural categories. Her networked camera lens is linked to a database and can identify creatures in its viewfinder. Although the animal/human orphans at the beginning of the game appear to be identified as *Homo sapiens*, the rhinoceros/human mechanics who run the Mammago garage shop appear in the photographic database as "rhino-sapiens," and they have Jamaican accents and dreadlocks and listen to reggae music. By contrast, the planetary authority called the Alpha Section is depicted, *Terminator*-style, as cyborg humanoids modeled after highly muscled white men. A subtle but pervasive cultural system that is based on race and species emerges in the game, and the animal/human hybrid minority characters are clearly oppressed. *Wired* magazine editor Chris Kohler, who examines a trend toward racial ambiguity in recent games, notes such ambiguity among the "good guys" in *Beyond Good & Evil*. Kohler describes Jade as racially ambiguous but most likely African American. Noting that Ubisoft intended Jade to reflect a diverse range of possible players, Kohler argues that the game's racial ambiguity could allow for better player identification.[11]

What is at stake in the game involves more than player identification. The diverse characters engage in activities at the bottom of the socioeconomic ladder, such as selling on the black-market, fixing vehicles, bartending, selling newspapers, or, at Jade's house, simply "being orphaned." Another "raced" example is Ming Tzu, a Chinese walrus who sells upgrades. In his scenes, game music shifts to Chinese stringed instruments, gongs, and Australian didgeridoos. These characters function outside the power structure of Alpha Section society and, in the case of Ming Tzu, are overtly stereotyped and depicted as human and animal hybrids. The Mammago brothers are Rhino humanoid (that is, less than human), and the muscled white "bad guys" remain *Homo sapiens*, separated through a legacy of racial and species discrimination dating back to the enlightenment. Thus, minority characters (like animals and hybrids) are identified with the natural world and with oppression (colonized by the DomZ).

Ubisoft's Michel Ancel has said that he intended the game to give the player "a promise of discovery" while playing.[12] The depictions of the characters, narrative, game interactions, and game spaces compel players to consider the values of equality, autonomy, and fairness. To Ancel, the design decisions that were made in the creation of *Beyond Good & Evil* "had kind of a political dimension. So for me, it has this serious aspect, it has this kind of depth, and it's very cool to see that people are sensitive to the fact that there could be a game with a message."[13]

Angry Birds

The bird soars through the air toward the structure. Will it hit and topple all of it (or most of it), or will it miss the mark? The smash casual game *Angry Birds* (Rovio 2009) posits a tropical island in which cartoon bird characters are angry at pigs for taking the birds' eggs. The pigs, presumably full, have taken refuge on unstable, collapsible structures, looking like pigeons sitting blissfully on structural framing. Players aim and fling the bird characters at the pigs using a slingshot styled catapult. The goal is to destroy the structures to gain points, wreak revenge, and advance to higher levels (figure 2.5). *Angry Birds* has gained international attention for its simplicity and popularity. The game and its expansions have been downloaded millions of times, and the game rapidly became a popular app for the iPad and other mobile devices. According to *Wired*, "Every day, users spend 200 million minutes—16 years every hour—playing the mobile game."[14]

Like all games, *Angry Birds* has values at play. Values that might be expressed by the game in its current state are interspecies differences, action, vengeance, destruction, humor, and violence. What if the game were modified to support the value of creativity instead of destruction?

Figure 2.5
Birds against pigs, from *Angry Birds* (Rovio 2009).

Perhaps after destroying the structure, the player would instead use the pieces to rebuild a new structure or build something that is higher or more decorative than other players. Even simple games like *Angry Birds* can be modified to include elements that promote the values to which designers, and their surrounding societies and cultures subscribe.

FarmVille

Now let's take a look at the popular social game, *FarmVille* (Zynga 2009a), a farming simulation game tied to existing social networks. Released in 2009 for Facebook and smartphones, *FarmVille* players manage their own virtual farm by planting, growing, and harvesting foods and trees (figure 2.6). In 2009, during *FarmVille*'s peak, over 80 million active users played the game every month.[15] *FarmVille* became so popular that many fan groups formed, including, for example, http://farmvilleart.com, started by one enthusiastic player, to gather player artworks created from the pixel-art-like layout of crops in fields (FarmVille Art 2009).

Players of *FarmVille* start off as a "field hand," receive a small plot of land, and build a farm on the plot. They are allowed to choose, plant, and harvest some simple crops, and eventually they may raise pigs and cows. Competitive players calculate comparative profits from the lists of available crops for purchase and determine which seeds create the highest earnings. Players who are not interested in winning might choose plants and flowers

Figure 2.6
A farm with a tidy arrangement of animals and crops, from *FarmVille* (Zynga 2009).

that they like. Players are permitted to purchase crops, trees, and farm animals and eventually to build structures on their expanding property. Harvesting crops or milking cows earns points, which are convertible to one of the game's currencies. As players advance, they are able to access more and more items with which to build or grow. As they gain experience, they may aspire to become Professors of Agriculture (level 15), Cream of the Crop (24), Sultan of Soil (26), Lord of the Plow (30), and so on, up to the original maximum level of 70. A year later, levels up to 120 were created, and some players hacked their way to levels in the tens of thousands.[16]

FarmVille includes two currencies: one is earned through completing tasks, and another augmented with real-world currencies. The game relies on repeat (perhaps obsessive) visits, and it rewards time-management skills. In one of the rare links to real-world behavior, certain digital crops ripen at different rates, and they must be harvested before they rot on the vine. Time is of the essence, and the game clock is ticking even when a player is offline. *FarmVille* champions the value of efficiency and time management. It does so by connecting to and amplifying habits such as the repetitive checking of Facebook. By encouraging repeated access to social networks, *FarmVille* promotes information sharing that allows companies to conduct data mining and click-tracking, and it increases their revenue from advertisements. Corporate values, in other words, lurk behind the other, more positive values the game depicts.[17]

FarmVille's game goals and reward structures are telling sources of its values. To begin with, nature must be commoditized: it has to have exchange value to matter in the game. Moreover, the values of community and friendship are highlighted by the way in which players are asked to gift items to other players. Negative values have a role as well. For example, the game constantly suggests that players get involved with their communities, constituting a sort of peer pressure. This pressure exacerbates the tensions that lie at the heart of the game—tensions that surround inclusivity and exclusivity. Gifts, notices, and the bonuses given to players who help each other both affirm friendship and commodify that friendship in the currency of the game. These values are not there by accident. "It's only about exploiting the players, and, yes, people report having fun with that kind of game," game designer Jonathan Blow has explained, criticizing the game. "Certain kinds of hardcore game players don't find much interest in *Farm-Ville*, but a certain large segment of the population does. But then when you look at the design process in that game, it's not about designing a fun game. It's not about designing something that's going to be interesting or a positive experience in any way—it's actually about designing something that's a negative experience."[18]

FarmVille is related to several other casual game phenomena in which user-created content and social interactions are the underlying focus of play. At least on the surface, its values appear to involve community, generosity, responsibility, good will, trust, friendship, and gender equity. Under the surface, however, two quandaries emerge. First, *FarmVille* relies on community, trust, and friendship, but the game also involves the exploitation of these values, and this exploitation often negates the positive values. Second, the values in *FarmVille* have little to do with the theme and graphics that are portrayed in the game. The game, in other words, does not reflect the values that players might expect to encounter in actual farming, such as sustainability, biological knowledge, land stewardship, tradition, and empathy. Indeed, the game actively undermines some of these values.

How can players balance or at least navigate values that conflict with each other? The designers of *FarmVille* have posited such conflicts to keep players engaged, and social interaction is fostered through direct encouragement of helping, assisting, gifting, and sharing. The game contains a tension between supporting these values and enforcing them. There is a difference. The legal scholar Ian Kerr has described "digital locks" that guard content (offering copyright protection, for instance) and extends this idea into digital content, where limits are put on the player or participant's actions.[19] Kerr might see places in digital games (like *FarmVille*) where players are deprived of personal growth as a real problem, because they do not permit players to act immorally. Kerr refers to this as "the automation of virtue": if we are forced to be moral, we might miss an opportunity to develop our own morality and make ethically meaningful choices. A contrary argument is offered by economists Richard H. Thaler and Cass R. Sunstein, authors of the 2008 book *Nudge: Improving Decisions about Health, Wealth, and Happiness*. They suggest that designers need to create a "choice architecture" to "nudge" players in beneficial directions without restricting freedom of choice.

Players in *FarmVille* are given frequent prompts to share data with friends or give a gift (say, free fuel) to a friend in need. Players also might be asked to help a friend who is not online to scare off foxes from their land to protect the harvest. Sharing or generosity is not enforced; players may decide not to share or gift. Yet the game also functions in a way that allows players to feel good about such acts of generosity. In *FarmVille*, players might experience less of a sense of empathy toward nature and more of a sense of empathy for their linked friends than they experience in *Flower*.

A player's reading of a text often departs from the game (its actions, narrative, representation, premise, and goals) in surprising ways. A key example of this in *FarmVille* is something fundamental: animals and crops are not nurtured in the way that they are in nondigital representation. In *FarmVille*, crops are planted and then harvested shortly thereafter, eradicating the need for good weather, sunshine, proper irrigation, weeding, and pest control. There are no daily care-giving tasks beyond the game level's requirements. There are no horrific farm accidents, no blights, and no cleaning of horse hooves. Players occasionally face crop ruin from neglect and understand that timing and attention affects both the farm and the context of play. These elements are more closely allied to the social ramifications of the game. What remains important is the player's virtual proximity to friends and the bonds that are woven through the game by that social interaction. The overhead perspective and grid-based design for the farm reflects a containable, controllable, and comprehensible space, an abstraction that lets players visualize where friends are cultivated as easily as the corn. The natural aspects of the game ultimately function as a mere skin, a geographical metaphor on a social network.

Call of Duty

Given that the *Call of Duty* (Activision 2003) games have sold more than 100 million copies, they can be considered a significant presence in the general media landscape. The first three *Call of Duty* games are played from the perspectives of Allied soldiers in World War II, and they convey a deep reverence for military heroism and sacrifice. Although all versions of the game are military shooters with similar core mechanics, the newer games typically tell warfare stories that are set in fictional near-future conflicts and occasionally portray the tactics of American and British military forces as self-defeating and morally questionable (figure 2.7).

It has been argued that the entertainment industry's reverential depictions of the Allied forces in World War II promote a pro-military consensus, especially at times when the moral authority of Western military actions is more ambiguous than it was in earlier times. For example, from the 1950s through the early 1970s, Americans were inundated with affirmations of the military's heroism through movies and television series about World War II. According to some media critics, this created a climate in which people were reluctant to criticize American involvement in the Vietnam War. The same critique can reasonably be applied to the first three *Call of Duty* games. They were released during the first three years of the second Iraq war, and they provided positive depictions of the American military at a time when many Americans viewed its deployment in the Middle East as both morally and strategically murky. Therefore, when we look at the

Figure 2.7
U.S. forces involved in a street conflict, from *Call of Duty 4: Modern Warfare* (Activision 2007), featuring conflicts in the Middle East and Russia in 2011.

values at play in these games, it is appropriate to focus on patriotic and militaristic values.

Analysis becomes more complicated, however, when the variability in players' interpretations of the games is considered. In interviews with *Call of Duty* players, one researcher found that American players who identified as politically conservative interpreted the games as an affirmation of "strong defense" values, which Joel Penney defines as "support of aggressive foreign policy as well a high regard for the military as an institution"(2010, 199).[20] On the other hand, players who were either politically liberal or not American ascribed different meanings to the games. For some, the reverential depiction of the Allied forces in the first three games suggests a contrast between good wars and bad wars: the moral clarity of the Allied mission in World War II made America's role in the Iraq war seem less noble by comparison. These players also suggested that the first three games affirm the value of multilateralism by immersing players in the roles of American, British, Soviet, Canadian, and Polish soldiers, thus carrying an implicit critique of America's relative unilateralism in the second Iraq war. This research on *Call of Duty* reveals that game design does not rigidly determine player experience. Rather, the game offers a range of plausible meanings. How a player is situated—personally, politically, and culturally—will influence the meanings (within the range of plausibility) that are absorbed.

Conclusion

The examples in this chapter provide a brief overview of the ways that values can be built into video games through their design features. The game *Ico* provides expressive environments and game mechanics and also promotes a sense of empathy and protection between players and Yorda by reinforcing the characters' dependence on and kindness toward each other at save states and in game scenarios. In *Angry Birds*, difference, action, vengeance, destruction, humor, and violence come into play. In *Flower*, players experience a nuanced kind of pleasure in exploring the landscape and the game's responsive aesthetics, and this generates contemplative play that highlights values of balance, sustainability, cooperation, and influence. *Beyond Good & Evil* offers rewards for nonviolence in the form of photographs, and the depictions of the characters, narrative, game interactions, and game spaces compel players to consider the values of equality, autonomy, and fairness. Economic imperatives can shape game values, as they do in *FarmVille*'s emphasis on sharing and commodifying one's experience, which fuel commercial social networking. *Call of Duty* seems to foster patriotic and militaristic values, but research reveals that conservative American players are likely to interpret the games differently from players with diverse political and social affiliations. Therefore, how a player is situated—personally, politically, and culturally—will influence which meanings (within the range of plausibility) are absorbed.

In this chapter, we show different ways values can emerge in games—sometimes evidently and obviously, at other times in ways subtly and less apparent. Players, too, introduce variations in their dissimilar ways of interpreting these values. Awareness that values—both positive and negative—are at play in games is an important first step for conscientious designers, but it's not enough. Our research suggests that those who wish to apply the principles of values-conscious design to their work have one critical need: a *systematic* way of approaching values in the design process. In this chapter, we swept through a range of examples to show the great variation in games where values manifest. Now, it is time to address the questions of where and how this happens with a deeper and more systematic approach. In the next chapter, we develop a framework of core game elements to serve as a scaffold for exploring these questions throughout the rest of the book.

3 Game Elements: The Language of Values

with Jonathan Belman

Games embody beliefs from a time and place, provide a sample of what is important to a particular group of makers and players, and offer us a way to understand what ideas and meanings are valuable. These beliefs may be investigated as part of the system on which a game operates—through rules, customs, player options, and more. In short, there are many elements in a game, and each affects how games access, represent, and foster particular values.

The many interrelated elements or dimensions of a game—narrative, interface, interactions, mechanics, and more—contribute to a coherent play experience. Any of these elements can have cultural, ethical, and political significance, even when they appear to be value-neutral.[1] Sometimes the values at play in an element are relatively obvious. It would be uncontroversial, for example, to argue that the representation of *Tomb Raider*'s (Core Design 1996) Lara Croft as a hypersexualized archeologist adventurer is deeply value-laden. By contrast, it is less immediately obvious how a particular game engine encourages violent play over nonviolent play.

This chapter presents a framework of fifteen elements that together constitute a game's semantic architecture, that is, the way that a game generates meanings:[2] These fifteen elements, by no means exhaustive, are offered with two purposes in mind. First, they can help designers locate specific ways in which values may be conveyed in games. Second, the elements can serve as a checklist of semantic architecture to encourage alertness toward aspects of a design-in-progress that have cultural, ethical, and political resonances, and as an aid throughout the design process. These fifteen elements are:

1. Narrative premise and goals
2. Characters
3. Actions in game

4. Player choice
5. Rules for interaction with other players and nonplayable characters
6. Rules for interaction with the environment
7. Point of view
8. Hardware
9. Interface
10. Game engine and software
11. Context of play
12. Rewards
13. Strategies
14. Game maps
15. Aesthetics

Although game elements are analytically distinct, they are not experienced individually by players, who are influenced by the context of the game; these elements tend to be thoroughly intertwined. Just as the word *shooting* means one thing in a conversation about gang violence and another in a conversation about photography, the shooting mechanic in the antiwar news game *September 12th* (Powerful Robot Games 2003) means something different from its counterpart in the commercial first-person shooter *Call of Duty 4: Modern Warfare* (Activision 2007). In general, elements that are considered independently may suggest a variety of meanings and values, but in the context of a game they may guide interpretation toward a limited range of meanings and values. We have selected the framework of game elements as a particular way of analyzing games because it useful for understanding the emergence of values. The framework is informed by our research with the Values at Play project, our experiences as game designers and educators, and much prior work in game studies and narrative studies.[3] Indeed, Values at Play belongs to a field-wide conversation about game elements. For example, Staffan Björk and Jussi Holopainen (2005) have examined game design patterns. Also of note are the mechanics, dynamics, and aesthetics (MDA) framework of Robin Hunicke, Marc LeBlanc, and Robert Zubek (2004); the formal and dramatic elements and system dynamics framework of Tracy Fullerton, Christopher Swain, and Steven Hoffman (2008); and Jesse Schell's (2008) lenses metaphor. Values at Play recognizes a debt to these works, which offer distinctive insights into how to parse games and how to analyze the complex activity of game design.

Building on these ideas, the framework of elements that we have developed is particularly useful in theory and practice when addressing the values that are at play in games. More detailed than most other models, ours allows for a nuanced reading of values in relation to each individual element and assumes that values also may emerge from interactions between two or more elements. The framework provides a structure for analyzing existing games and designing new ones. After briefly describing each element, we present innovative or exciting applications of both in the service of Values at Play.

1. Narrative Premise and Goals

What is the story? What goals or motivations drive the playable or player character (that is, the character controlled by the person playing the game, shortened to PC)? Who or what is the playable character pursuing, and what happens along the way? How are the events ordered? What will the playable character have accomplished when the game is "beaten" or "won"? Are players paying attention to the narrative as they play? The narrative element can be more or less integral to the overall play experience. For example, the narrative premise of *Super Mario Bros.* (Nintendo 1985) is Mario's quest to rescue Princess Toadstool from her kidnapper, Bowser. However, aside from short, generic, and repetitive noninteractive scenes, nothing in the game makes direct reference to the princess's kidnapping or gives the player a reason to consider it an important part of minute-to-minute gameplay. Players might engross themselves in the game without giving thought to the nature of the princess's plight. Games can be engaging when narrative is cursory or even absent, but narrative can be an obvious site for values-rich content, motivation, and context.

Illustrative Game: *September 12th*
September 12th (Powerful Robot Games 2003) begins with a cryptic set of instructions that read, in part, as follows: "You can't win and you can't lose.... The rules are deadly simple. You can shoot. Or not. This is a simple model you can use to explore some aspects of the War on Terror." The instructions also provide the means for identifying the game's two categories of nonplayable characters: the men who are wearing keffiyeh (the traditional headdress of Arab men) and carrying guns are terrorists, and the people who are in robes and skullcaps or headscarves are civilians (figure 3.1).

The game world is a busy desert marketplace where terrorists are spotted here and there among civilians. The player controls a targeting reticule that can be positioned anywhere in the market, and left-clicking fires a missile at the reticule's location. Inferring a narrative premise from this set-up is

Figure 3.1
A "deadly simple" narrative posits players as shooters, from *September 12th* (Powerful Robot Games 2003).

not as straightforward as it usually is in mainstream games. The playable character represents the American side in the war on terror, and someone familiar with the conventions of video games probably would assume that the playable character is supposed to use missiles to eliminate terrorists in the marketplace. However, when the player fires on the terrorists, the explosion is so large and the crowd so thick that both terrorists and civilians are killed. In the aftermath of the attack, people around the explosion begin mourning, and some become terrorists themselves. Firing a missile typically creates more terrorists than it kills.

What will the playable character accomplish when the game is "beaten"? The only sense in which the game can be beaten is if the player realizes the futility of the playable character's one-dimensional approach to fighting terrorism. *September 12th* inverts the conventional approach to narrative in video games by encouraging the player to recognize that something is flawed in the assumptions underlying the playable character's view of the world and something is tragic and self-defeating in his quest. This might spur players to critique the premises of the real-world war on terror.

2. Characters

Can playable characters be customized or selected? If they can, how is this done, and what options are provided? What are the characters' attributes and characteristics? What are the characteristics and roles of nonplayable characters? In some games, characters are predefined, but in others, the importance of character emerges outside of its purely narrative components. Think of Chrono from *Chrono Trigger* (Square 1995), Link from the *The Legend of Zelda* series (Nintendo et al. 1986) (figure 3.2), and Gordon Freeman from *Half-Life* (Valve 1998). These characters all are examples of a silent protagonist or tabula rasa, and all have garnered much acclaim in the gaming community because they play active roles in game narratives and seem to act as expressive vessels through which the player moves through the game. To the player, such characters define themselves more in terms of their player-controlled actions than in their dialogue or predetermined storylines.

SHODAN (Sentient Hyper-Optimized Data Access Network) is the antagonist in the *System Shock* (Irrational Games et al. 1999) series and drives the game narratives. She has earned a spot in gaming lore for her sinister demeanor and the way in which plot twists in *System Shock 2* are linked to realizations about her character. The Nameless One in *Planetscape: Torment* (Black Isle Studios 1999) provides a good example for a playable character that propels a game, because the narrative is concerned with having the

Figure 3.2
Link fighting, from *The Legend of Zelda: Twilight Princess* (Nintendo 1986).

character/player gradually discover who he or she is. Mario the plumber is not nearly as complex as these characters but is a perennial favorite as an everyman turned hero.

It is helpful to examine the kind of relationship that a game intends to establish between players and characters. For example, to what extent will the player feel complicit in the playable character's actions? Will the player relate to playable characters, be revolted by them, or react with some other emotional response?

Illustrative Games: *Portal* and *Layoff*

In the *Portal* (Valve 2007) first-person puzzle game series, there are two characters—GLaDOS (Genetic Lifeform and Disk Operating System) and Chell, the silent protagonist player character. The GLaDOS artificially intelligent system is responsible for maintenance and testing within the Aperture Science facility as Chell, a former test subject, tries to escape the center (figure 3.3). At first, GLaDOS is merely an instructional voice that monitors and directs players as they move forward in their "testing procedures." Yet even early in the game, the instructions that she broadcasts across the facility start to take on sinister aspects. At one point, GLaDOS cautions, "Before we start, however, keep in mind that although fun and learning are the primary goals of all enrichment center activities, serious injuries may occur." As players move forward, GLaDOS tries to intimidate the player into failure or trick the player into succeeding fewer times. To entice the player character forward, GLaDOS promises parties and a reward of cake for finishing the challenges, while warning the player character of her impending demise: "Cake and grief counseling will be available at the conclusion of the test." By her own admission, however, GLaDOS is a liar. To add to player stress (and humor in the game), GLaDOS frequently taunts the player: "Please note that we have added a consequence for failure. Any contact with the chamber floor will result in an 'unsatisfactory' mark on your official testing record followed by death. Good luck!"

In the first *Portal*, GLaDOS eventually is exposed as a corrupted AI that employed neurotoxins to kill all of the prior scientists in the lab except Chell. At the end of *Portal*, Chell destroys some of GLaDOS's hardware, including one of her personality core spheres (her "morality core"). As Chell dismembers GLaDOS's hardware, a new portal is formed, and both Chell and pieces of GLaDOS are seen lying outside the Aperture Science facility. In the game sequel *Portal 2*, GLaDOS is back, accidentally activated by Chell and a positive artificial intelligence named Wheatley. Wheatley ends up being tempted by power and greed and betrays Chell.

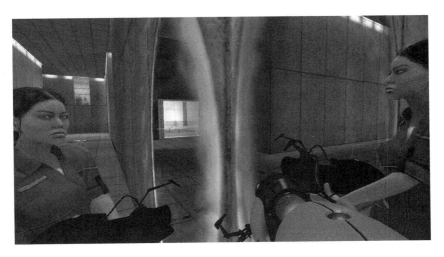

Figure 3.3
Chell, from *Portal* (Valve 2007).

GLaDOS in *Portal* promises freedom, autonomy, and choice but is critical and cruel to the player character and is intent on her destruction. The player character Chell reacts against these restrictive values in what becomes a clever battle of good versus evil. Chell must rely on creativity and trust in her own abilities to acquire her freedom. When the player character Chell is compared to GLaDOS's manipulative and malicious behavior, Chell the player character seems honest, clear, genuine, and in the right.

The casual game *Layoff* (Tiltfactor Lab 2009) is designed to elicit empathy in players toward characters in the game (and toward the real-world people who are represented by those characters). Unlike *Hush* (Jamie Antonisse and Devon Johnson 2007), which we will discuss in detail in section 3, *Layoff* elicits a different kind of empathy. It is a matching game that resembles others in the genre such as *Bejeweled* (Popcap Games 2001). In *Bejeweled*, players swap adjacent gems on a playing board to create horizontal or vertical sets of three or more identical gems. When sets are created, their component gems disappear from the board and are replaced by new gems falling from the top.

In *Layoff*, players take on the role of "corporate management," tasked with cutting jobs during a financial crisis (figure 3.4). Each icon in this matching game represents a worker. When the player matches sets of three or more workers, they fall off the bottom end of the board into an "unemployment office." From management's perspective, the workers are interchangeable parts that can be swapped and terminated to save money. But the game is designed to challenge this perspective that a worker is only a cog in a machine. Each worker has a short biography that pops up when his or her icon is selected. For example:

Jaime, 39, is a client relationship manager at a small outsourcing company. This is a new job in Boston, and Jaime likes it very much except for the climate. Jaime works from home on Fridays to ease financial pressure or childcare, but the manager is possibly going to cut all employees down to a 4-day workweek.

In *Layoff*, a bond of empathy is created not only between the player and the playable character, representing management, but rather between the player and nonplayable characters, representing the workers being laid off. (By contrast, in *Hush*, discussed in section 3, players do seem to experience a sample of the same broad class of emotions experienced by the playable character). Even so, in *Layoff*, players probably do not feel exactly what workers actually feel when they lose their jobs. Instead, they might experience indignation at the callousness of the management toward the workers, or sorrow for the people who have lost their jobs in a bad economy.

Figure 3.4
Individual characters in *Layoff* fostered empathy during an overwhelming financial crisis (Tiltfactor Lab 2009).

This is what psychologists call reactive empathy—an emotional reaction to another person's situation that does not mirror that person's own emotional state.

Layoff and *Portal* are excellent models of games that create meaningful bonds between players and characters to establish a personal connection with a larger issue or event.

3. Actions in Game

What can the player do (or cause playable characters to do) in a game? Most contemporary mainstream games enable a limited set of playable character actions. In games such as *Call of Duty* (Activision 2003), *Angry Birds* (Rovio 2009), and sports games, common actions emerge, including shooting, fighting, running, driving, and sports-related actions (such as batting or jumping). This does not mean that a game where the playable character primarily shoots a gun, for example, will necessarily be clichéd or derivative. *September 12th* is an excellent example of a game in which a conventional action takes on new meanings when placed in a new context. We have been excited by the tremendous expressive possibilities of games that are built around less conventional actions.

Illustrative Games: *Three Player Chess, Waking Mars,* and *Hush*

Traditional chess, in which two players compete for dominance of the board by capturing each other's pieces, has conventionally been interpreted as an allegory for war. *Three Player Chess* (Catlow 2001) subverts the mechanics (and allegory) of traditional chess by introducing a third player whose goal is to create a state of peace between the other two players (figure 3.5).

Two players in *Three Player Chess* control either the black or white "power pieces" (kings, queens, knights, and rooks). The third player controls all pawns and uses the pawns to run interference between the other two players, preventing them from capturing each other's pieces. If no pieces are captured for five turns, grass begins to grow on the board, covering the black and white checks. If no pieces are captured for twenty turns, the entire board becomes covered in grass, representing a victory for the pawns and, in the realm of this game, world peace.

The designer said that the game was inspired by the second Iraq war, when the peaceful protests of ordinary people (pawns) presented a counterpoint to the belligerence of power players in the George W. Bush administration. The designer asked a question: under what conditions could nonpower players (pawns) achieve victory over power players? An answer

Figure 3.5
Chess game, from *Three Player Chess* (Catlow 2001).

to this question is suggested by player actions that offer a pacifist alternative to the martial allegory of traditional chess.

Three Player Chess subverts traditional chess by providing the pawns with
a pacifist role. Values emerge from the twist on a traditional game. Game
actions instigate values at any time, however, and do so even when they are
there merely to support the game concept.

In *Waking Mars* (Tiger Style 2012), the year is 2097, four years after alien
life forms were discovered in Mars caves. Players play the game as exploring scientist Liang and fly through the caves, cataloging and discovering
the new life forms (figure 3.6). Players plant alien seeds, foster their growth
by collecting resources and distributing them accordingly, and then move
on to animal-like organisms. In some cases, players must bring life forms
to life; in others, the forms must be managed. Players check their progress
through a Biomass score, which increases by planting flora and oversee-
ing the life cycle of fauna. Players create ecosystems of their own designs
and strive to achieve high biomass and build balanced systems. To reach
a balanced system, players must discover states of equilibrium or risk creating unbalanced and unproductive relationships between the organisms

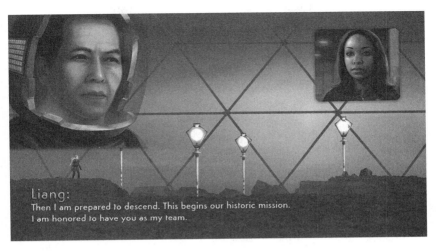

Liang:
Then I am prepared to descend. This begins our historic mission.
I am honored to have you as my team.

Figure 3.6
Liang, from *Waking Mars*, working to revive the planet (Tiger Style 2012).

that will not generate enough biomass. The goal of the game is to discover the secrets of Mars's past by bringing the dormant plants to life, but this will work only if the ecosystem is robust. The notion of balance infuses the game: some plants grow in basic soils, others in acidic soils; some organisms are immobile, others are mobile; some organisms are constructive organisms and breed offspring, others are destructive. Patience is required in this relatively slow-paced game as players solve puzzles about which life forms are symbiotic with others. Instead of rewarding players for winning or conquering, the game rewards players for considering cause and effect and, over a longer time period than typically is designed into a casual game, it also credits players' attention to sustainability.

Hush (Jamie Antonisse and Devon Johnson 2007) uses a timing/matching mechanic to immerse the player in the role of the playable character, a Rwandan Tutsi mother hiding with her baby in a hut during the 1994 genocide (figure 3.7). Players play as a mother who sings a lullaby to pacify her baby as soldiers pass by outside the window. If the lullaby falters, the baby begins to cry, and the soldiers may discover the hiding place.

Hush's creators, Jamie Antonisse and Devon Johnson, were conscientious designers who found ways to express values through their game. The player "sings" the lullaby by typing it at the precise rhythm indicated by on-screen prompts. Players have reported that as they miss notes in the lullaby, the baby's cries grow louder, and the soldiers come nearer, they

Figure 3.7
The player actions generating incredible tension and empathy, from *Hush* (Jamie
Antonisse and Devon Johnson 2007).

feel an escalating sense of tension and dread. The game won the 2008 Better Game contest, where judges said that they were amazed by the anxiety
that the game causes. In demo after demo of this game, across audiences,
players are moved. After watching the game being played, people approach
the demonstrator or player to say that this was the first time they had had
such an emotional reaction to a game. They consistently felt a strong sense
of empathy for the mother. This is an example of what psychologists call
parallel empathy, where one person feels emotions that are akin to those
felt by another person.[4] A game can provide players with only an extremely
limited experience of a situation this dire, but *Hush* creates an empathetic
bond between player and playable character.

4. Player Choice

Unlike most other media, games can provide players an opportunity for
choice. Many games channel players down a relatively linear path from
beginning to end, with determined events that must happen on each level.

Some games, however, provide choices that significantly influence the play experience, and in some cases the choices have a moral valence. For example, the *Mass Effect* (Bioware 2007) games allow players to approach situations as a compassionate, conciliatory, and altruistic "paragon" or as a ruthless, belligerent, and self-serving "renegade." Choice of play style greatly affects interactions and relationships with nonplayable characters and also determines how the storyline unfolds.

From a values perspective, what does it mean to offer or withhold these kinds of choices? Games like *Mass Effect* equally incentivize "good" and "evil" choices, and they might be considered morally relativistic. It could be that players experience them as a kind of sandbox for moral play, allowing them to explore ethical issues in a setting where real-world consequences do not apply.

Illustrative Games: *Star Wars: Knights of the Old Republic, The McDonald's Videogame,* and *Spent*

The *Star Wars: Knights of the Old Republic* (KOTOR) (Bioware 2003) role-playing games are similar to the *Mass Effect* games in that players choose to follow either the "light path" (in which the playable character's behavior is motivated by compassion, mercy, and self-sacrifice) or the "dark path" (in which the playable character is driven by hatred and lust for power) (figure 3.8). Depending on path chosen for one of the three player character classes, the games' stories progress differently, and the playable characters develop different powers.

Figure 3.8
In *Star Wars: Knights of the Old Republic* (KOTOR), players may choose a dark path or a light path (Bioware 2003).

The *KOTOR* games present intriguing moral choices, but players do not necessarily make their decisions using moral criteria. One player might act ruthlessly to acquire dark-side powers because doing so introduces entertaining mechanics. Another player might act virtuously to unlock the light-side powers. So the moral character of the game could depend significantly on how the player decides to engage with it,[5] and players do likely question their identities and responsibilities in gameplay.

The McDonald's Videogame (Molleindustria 2006) offers a different approach to player choice. This is a business simulation like *Railroad Tycoon* (MicroProse 1990) or *The Movies* (Lionhead Studios 2005) in which the player micromanages various aspects of a commercial enterprise. The game description text on the *McDonald's* videogame website, written from the point of view of Ronald McDonald, admits that the business has had "glitches" in terms of deforestation, food poisoning, and so on and has negatively affected society and the environment. Unlike most casual games, *The McDonald's Videogame* is designed to convey an argument on the nature of capitalism. Starting in the year 2000, players work through successive years to raise revenue. Players need to supervise all areas of the fast-food chain, including agriculture, feedlots, restaurants, and boardrooms (figure 3.9). Because choices are limited, destroying strips of rainforest to

Figure 3.9
The player choices in *The McDonald's Videogame* reflect the nature of contemporary global business practices: the player must destroy South American rainforests to farm for McDonald's (Molleindustria 2006).

produce grazing land for cattle, for example, is inevitable. Restaurant traffic can be controlled by marketing campaigns. Ian Bogost analyzes the play experience:

The McDonald's Videogame mounts a procedural rhetoric about the necessity of corruption in the global fast food business, and the overwhelming temptation of greed, which leads to more corruption. In order to succeed in the long-term, the player must use growth hormones, he must coerce banana republics, and he must mount PR and lobbying campaigns. Furthermore, the temptation to destroy indigenous villages, launch bribery campaigns, recycle animal parts, and cover up health risks is tremendous, although the financial benefit from doing so is only marginal.[6]

The game creates an interesting tension between player choice (players can choose whether to engage in the most injurious business practices) and a general propensity toward running up the score. Players switch between a farm that supplies food to McDonald's (where deforestation must happen to keep up with growing land needs), a feed lot (where cows are fattened and players attempt to stop disease), a McDonald's restaurant (where inefficient workers should be fired—"eliminate the weak links"), and corporate headquarters (where the board of directors and the public relations office develops countermeasures against company detractors).

In most games, the choices that players make may be almost exclusively determined by what awards them higher scores (or whatever the game uses as markers of achievement or progress). Similarly, in the context of capitalist venture, player behaviors may be directed almost exclusively toward the goal of higher profits, and in some instances may find exploitation, bribery, and deceit almost irresistibly pragmatic behaviors. By immersing players in the decision-making processes of fast-food executives, the game offers a cogent critique of prevailing political and economic values.

Spent (McKinney 2011) also fosters thought-provoking tensions between player choices, but it does so by limiting possibility to unfavorable options (figure 3.10). The game offers players realistic but difficult decisions that people would face when living on $1,000 per month in or around Durham, North Carolina. Made for the Urban Ministries of Durham, the game offers dilemmas that lead people to seek social or financial help. The goal is to end the month with some funds remaining, but interruptions such as accidents or health issues crop up and threaten to upend the player. Players learn how quickly shifts in jobs, apartments, and medical care can lead to homelessness and poverty.

"You'd never need help, right?" the game asks the player at the start. Players enter the game by clicking "Prove It: Accept the Challenge." Statistics

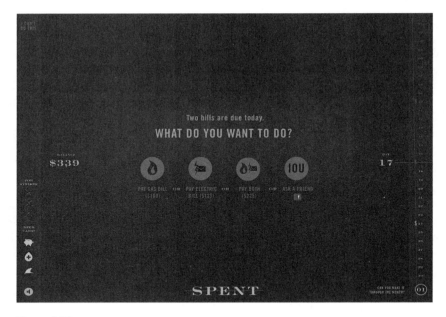

Figure 3.10
Spent demonstrates how close most Americans are to homelessness (McKinney 2011).

open the game to position the player's point of view: 14 million Americans are unemployed, and you are a single parent. Can you make it through the month? The options are "Find a Job" or "Exit." From there on, players choose from limited options, such as applying for a job as a restaurant server, warehouse worker, or temporary office worker. Temps have to take an in-game typing test. Restaurant servers have to purchase their uniforms. Most groceries are too costly for the monthly budget.

The game offers real-world feedback from data based on the Durham area. For example, the player can choose to live closer to work, where the rent is much higher, or live farther away, where transportation costs are higher. After players choose an option, the game displays a message acknowledging that "you and 12 million other American households" spend too much on housing.

5. Rules for Interaction with Other Players or Nonplayable Characters

Values are often conspicuously at play in the ways that games afford and regulate interactions with other players or nonplayable characters. Sometimes nonplayable characters offer hints or permit interesting interactions for finding clues or trading. The single-player game series *Fable* (Microsoft 2004) has deeper-than-average development of nonplayable characters, but there are many good examples of meaningful interactions with nonplayable characters. In multiplayer games, customs and rules that are unique to the gaming community can govern interactions (the context of play is more fully detailed as an element later in this chapter). Some games create unwelcoming spaces for new players. In contrast, the massively multiplayer online role-playing game (MMORPG) *City of Heroes* (NCsoft 2004) encourages cooperative relationships between new and experienced players. The game uses a "sidekick system" that provides incentives to both higher- and lower-level characters to play as a team. This relatively straightforward set of rule changes can completely reframe relationships between experts and novices. By tinkering with the rules for interaction with other players or nonplayable characters, designers can put values like cooperation, generosity, and altruism into play or can adjust these rules to affirm more individualistic values like competition and self-sufficiency.

Illustrative Games: Rock, Paper, Scissors Tag and *Journey*

Celia Pearce, Tracy Fullerton, Janine Fron, and Jacqueline Ford Morie have described an event called New Games Day, where students, faculty, and staff at the University of Southern California revived some of the games created by the experimental New Games Movement of the 1970s.[7] Working with traditional games, the team's "new" New Games featured large-scale activities that incorporated physicality, trust, and cooperation. Their description of rock, paper, scissors tag provides an excellent example of how changing the rules for interactions between players can reconceptualize the competitive ethos that often is associated with sport and play (figure 3.11):

By far, the group favorite was a game called Rock-Paper-Scissors Tag. In this game, two teams face off across a line. On the count of three, each group shows rock, paper, or scissors, having huddled beforehand to decide on a strategy. The team that shows the losing sign turns and runs to their home base, about fifteen feet behind. The team that shows the winning sign gives chase. Any person tagged by the winning team transfers to that team for the next round of play. The key to the game lies in the fluidity of the teams. Although you may have started on Team 1, soon you will be on Team 2, then back to Team 1, and so on. The game goes on until there is only one team or until everyone is too exhausted to continue.[8]

Many traditional sports use a team-based competitive framework that categorizes other players as either enemy or ally, and that categorization is maintained from the beginning of the game until the end. This team building can create strong bonds among players and animosity toward

Figure 3.11
A version of rock, paper, scissors tag being played at Dartmouth College.

opponents.[9] However, when players switch teams frequently, as in rock, paper, scissors tag, the distinction between allies and adversaries becomes too ephemeral to "stick" in the same way that it does in traditional competitive sports. In the words of Pearce and her colleagues, the alternative approach to competitive play "encourages a global allegiance to the play of the game itself rather than to the success of any particular team."[10]

Journey (thatgamecompany 2012) is a PlayStation 3 game that positions the player as a lone robed figure wearing a scarf and wandering in a vast desert (figure 3.12). Players find themselves traveling on a quest to a distant mountain to discover the history of a once vibrant culture that occupied the land. In each level, the player may encounter one other player who might temporarily connect to their game. The players can see, meet, and help each other, but they can communicate only through musical patterns of singing, and they are paired anonymously. Players can help each other only by showing each other paths or helping change one another's scarves.

The chime that creates the music transforms found cloth into magical red cloth, which allows the player to float for a time. If players finish a level together, they can stay together for the next. Players can be distinguished by their unique symbols that appear in the air as they sing or are marked on their robes. The design of the game fosters cooperation between players without requiring it and removes competition. Because a player can be helpful to the other player but cannot harm the player, player interaction

Figure 3.12
Journey's haunting spiritual quest (thatgamecompany 2012).

tends to be collaborative and profound. Designer Jenova Chen has noted that some playtesters cry after completing the game. At thatgamecompany's Web forum for the game, players discuss crying in depth. One player notes, "The one thing that really amazes me though, journey [sic] doesn't trigger my desire to win or to be better than someone. Something that happens in nearly every other game."[11]

6. Rules for Interaction with the Environment

What types of interactions does the game afford between playable characters and the nonsentient aspects of the game world (i.e., those aspects of the game world that are not characters)? What resources are available? What types of interactions are incentivized through the game's rules and the capacity of the artificial intelligence system? Is the player rewarded for exploring or appreciating, for depleting resources or replenishing them, or for destroying the game world or nurturing it?

Illustrative Games: *StarCraft* and *Trash Tycoon*
StarCraft (1998), a game series created by Blizzard Entertainment after its successful *Warcraft* game (1994), is a real-time strategy game set in the twenty-fifth century, where three species fight for dominance—the insect-like Zerg, the Protoss (a humanoid species with psychic abilities), and

Terrans (humans exiled from Earth). In many strategy games like *StarCraft*, players continually harvest the game world's resources for raw materials to build military hardware, buildings, and so on, and they are given no mechanism through which to replenish those resources. It would be a stretch to say that games like *StarCraft* inculcate anti-environmentalist values, but such games do little to promote the value of sustainability.

The *FarmVille*-like Facebook game *Trash Tycoon* (Guerillapps 2011) provides an example of a game that is compatible with sustainability (figure 3.13). The game's core concept is "upcycling" or converting waste to new materials or products that are of higher quality and better for the environment. Players clean up a trash-strewn city, build facilities like paper recyclers and glass smelters, and sell the products to earn funds to build new facilities and upgrade existing ones. Along the way, they earn badges and rewards for reaching sustainability milestones. The Plastic Master bronze badge, for example, is earned by creating twenty items with recycled plastic.

On an abstract level, the rules of *Trash Tycoon* are nearly identical to those of many mainstream strategy games. The player harvests resources (in this case, trash) and processes them into products that facilitate progress

Figure 3.13
Upcycling in *Trash Tycoon* addresses the aftermath of trash (Guerillapps 2011).

toward in-game goals. This is not mechanically different from harvesting minerals in *StarCraft*, for example, to be processed into siege tanks. The narrative of *Trash Tycoon* reskins the conventional rule sets of strategy games to engender a very different set of values.[12] The issue of producing trash in the first place is not addressed, however, which calls into question the effectiveness of reskinning a commonly accepted and successful game model for a social-impact game when the root of the problem remains.

7. Point of View

As in other forms of media, point of view in games shapes how viewers and participants experience the world that is being presented. How do players view the playable character? Do they survey the game world from a first- or third-person perspective? Do players take on the view of a certain character, or are they controlling the situation from a God's-eye, top-down view? Is it something in between or both? Point of view may partially determine how players understand themselves in relation to other players, nonplayable characters, and the game world and may also influence how they conceive their own agency. For example, a game in which playable characters are controlled from a top-down perspective may suggest that players occupy the role of a "god" or "master." In contrast, a first-person perspective may encourage greater identification with playable characters. Even within one point of view (such as third-person), there are wide variations in interpretation. The vast majority of the *Uncharted* (Naughty Dog 2007) games, for example, are third person, but the camera is dynamic. Most of the games implement an over-the-shoulder camera (common in games like *Resident Evil 4* (Capcom 2005) and *Gears of War* (Epic Games 2006), but some platforming sections have the camera pull back so that the game effectively become a side-scroller. Other platforming sections in *Uncharted* have the camera lie in front of the playable character as he continually runs toward it while something chases him from behind, as in *Crash Bandicoot* (Naughty Dog 1996). Subtleties in point of view, such as camera position, make a difference. Even though all three of *Uncharted*'s camera placements are third person in the broadest sense, they encourage different gameplay, a different relation to the playable character, and a different play experience.

Illustrative Games: *Tomb Raider* and *Mirror's Edge*

The *Tomb Raider* (Eidos 1996) games have used a conventional third-person perspective in which the camera hovers behind Lara Croft, the series' iconic playable character. Although the camera often zooms out to accommodate segments of gameplay that require a wider view, it usually returns to just behind Lara, offering what many critics have argued is a voyeuristically satisfying view of her body (figure 3.14).

The critic Mike Ward notes the significance of seeing Lara from the back during gameplay: the voyeur's pleasure depends on being able to look without being seen.[13] None of this means that the third-person perspective is necessarily sexualizing or objectifying. But with the context provided by Lara's clothing (typically tight shorts and a tank top) and her proportions (large hips and breasts on an otherwise slender frame), the effect is unambiguously sexual.

Compare this to how point of view is used in *Mirror's Edge* (EA Digital Illusions CE 2008), another action-adventure game with a female playable character. Players see the action from a first-person perspective through the eyes of its playable character, a courier named Faith who works with antiauthoritarian rebels in a totalitarian society (figure 3.15). When she runs, the distance moves quickly forward. When she jumps, the player's view of the world rises and then falls. We do not see much of Faith's body in gameplay. Instead, the focus is more on her actions, which are represented through shifts in her field of vision as she moves. Whereas the *Tomb Raider* games present a strong female character who seems at least partly designed

Figure 3.14
Camera controls highlighting third-person perspective in games such as *Tomb Raider* can offer a voyeur's pleasure (Eidos 1996).

Figure 3.15
Faith, from *Mirror's Edge* (EA Digital Illusions CE 2008).

for male pleasure, *Mirror's Edge* offers a female action hero who is, semantically speaking, less paradoxical.

8. Hardware

Game hardware shapes how designers think about games. The hardware—the core capacity of system memory, the speed of graphics processors, and the physical device of the mouse, controller, or keyboard—frames the possibilities of designers' imaginations.[14] With each advance in hardware, new types of games are possible. This has been true throughout the history of electronic and digital games. The very early game *Tennis for Two* (Higinbotham 1958) used an oscilloscope as a visual monitor. In 1998, Nintendo bundled a "biosensor" with *Tetris 64* (Amtex 1998), and in 2010, it offered a "vitality sensor" that monitors a player's pulse. In the 2002 game *Rez* (Sega 2001), designed by Tetsuya Mizuguchi, players fly three-dimensionally (using a "rail shooter" convention in 3D space) into a seemingly endless tunnel filled with sound, light, and enemies. Always flying forward, players fire at enemies, gain points, and create electronic music with the sounds they are creating. The game was intended to be played with an additional piece of hardware called "the trance vibrator." This hardware was designed to be worn on the body to draw even more senses into the action and create a synesthetic experience.

Illustrative Game: *Dance Central 2*

Dance Central 2 (Harmonix 2011) embodies some interesting features that are made possible by the Xbox Kinect hardware, which offers a camera and infrared interface to allow hands-free, accurate control of items on screen. Whereas older dance games used pads to detect foot movements, Kinect hardware allows *Dance Central 2* to respond to a player's entire body (figure 3.16). The game can track one body or several, monitor bodies in motion in a 3D area, offer simultaneous two-player battles, and provide the ability to monitor and reward dancing to challenging choreography.

The accuracy of the body detection allows players to focus on more creative aspects of dancing, such as style, precision, and timing. The game thus encourages actual dancing rather than dancing "for the game" or making moves solely to get the controller to respond. Additionally, the game's use of its camera data to provide fun, fast-paced replays of the dancers highlights the individual dancing rather than only the game's characters. This accuracy shapes the values of the game by allowing players to express creativity and individuality.

9. Interface

Interface refers to attributes of the software and hardware that mediate players' interactions with the game. Interfaces are constructs of hardware (such

Figure 3.16
Kinect hardware enables a new breed of dancing game in *Dance Central 2* (Harmonix 2011).

as in the Kinect) and software, which are the modes through which players interact with the game world. Both physical and on-screen elements shape the player experience. Although these are often assumed to be value-neutral, they may shape the play experience in value-rich ways. For example, a hardware interface that allows physically disabled people to play might be said to affirm the values of inclusiveness and accessibility. A software interface that allows for easy communication between players might affirm the value of cooperation by facilitating collaborative tactical play.

Illustrative Game: *Leela* and *[giantJoystick]*

Often, video games feature fast movements and frenetic decision making. Deepak Chopra's *Leela* (THQ 2011a) is the opposite type of game. Using an Xbox Kinect (or Nintendo Wii, although the Wii version is not as full-featured), players learn seven meditations and movements that help focus the mind on parts of the body where the seven chakras lie (figure 3.17). The idea that games might offer a spiritual or religious connection is very old, originating in the origins of games six to eight thousand years ago. A digital interface to religion and spirituality, however, seems rather new. In the "Play" section of the *Leela* gaming experience, players play games that target one of their chakras and use subtle movements to stimulate the chakras.

The navel chakra, for example, is supposedly stimulated as players aim and gather virtual fireballs (the navel chakra's element) to blast floating ore.

Figure 3.17
The interface of *Leela* involves the body as well as the mind (THQ 2011).

The chakras can be stimulated in sequences, or the player can work on his or her personal mandala. The look of the game—particularly in the "Mandala" section—is psychedelic, with trancelike interactive compositions that feature repeating patterns, manipulable fractals, and shifting colors. In the "Reflect" area of *Leela*, players use the game as a platform for guided meditation or as an accompaniment to silent meditation. The Kinect actually measures a player's breathing, for example, and the game displays a representation of the player's breath to offer feedback. Chopra is interested in healing and the intersection of science, consciousness, and spirituality and has created a successful game that mirrors in a compelling way some internal processes for which other interfaces would be inadequate.

The coauthor of this book, Mary Flanagan, has created an interactive sculpture called *[giantJoystick]* (2006) that embodies the value of cooperation by modifying the user interface of classic Atari 2600 games like *Asteroids* and *Breakout*. The original incarnations of these games are deeply engaging but can become an isolating pursuit: they shift players' attention toward the action onscreen and away from friends in the physical environment. To change the value of individuality to the value of cooperation and particularly to foster cooperation among strangers, Flanagan changed a specific element of the design—in this case, the scale of the user interface. By making the joystick enormous—it is over 10 feet tall and requires steps

Figure 3.18
The interactive, ten-foot sculpture *[giantJoystick]* makes the familiar unfamiliar with a significant shift in interface scale (Mary Flanagan 2006).

to mount the sculpture—the play experience is transformed (figure 3.18). First, players report transitioning to a childlike state of feeling small again by the sheer scale of the play object: *[giantJoystick]* brings a feeling of wonder to players. Second, scale fosters a childlike fascination with the work but also determines how people interact in play. Visitors cannot easily play games by themselves with *[giantJoystick]*. One person (or sometimes more than one) moves the stick, while another presses the fire button by jumping on it. Through its shift in scale, the work highlights the spatial and social role of the interface. *[giantJoystick]* itself becomes the game and the site for interpersonal communication. With the new interface, classic games become a joyous celebration of collaborative fun. *[giantJoystick]* redefines technological conventions by recognizing the physicality and arbitrary nature of interfaces themselves. Flanagan's controller connects real people in real space, a phenomenon that is quickly becoming an emerging domain for digital games as new hardware and interface technologies involve the body and evolve the nature of digital gameplay.

10. Game Engine and Software

How does a particular software constraint or game engine affect what goes into a game? The affordances of the engine or codebase allow a game to appear and act as it does. Game engines—software frameworks that are used to create games—are often touted for their new features, such as the novelty of the physics engine (rendering, textures, environment, particle systems, lighting, and frame rate), networking ability (multiplayer, chat), and customizability (using tools such as editors). Constraints that are built into the software or the game engine can shape the content and values in a game. In the domain of first-person shooters, the game engines created for *Wolfenstein 3D* (id Software 1992) and *Doom* (id Software 1993) set the stage for many conventions that are still in use in 3D gameplay. The engines highly constrained physical interactions, for example: players typically run, jump, duck, and shoot, but they might not reach out with virtual hands to touch something. Players cannot pet a dog, for example, or reach with someone else to carry something. These constraints shape design decisions.

Ragdoll physics, for example, is one example where "what could be done" became a default technique in many 3D games. With ragdoll physics, the animation is computationally generated, allowing the game to avoid "canned" or predrawn sequences. Ragdoll physics has been used primarily in death scenes, which become more "realistic" because bodies fall in unique ways. Other game conventions also have emerged simply because of the limitations of the game engine. For example, game characters "pick up" objects mostly by running over or shooting at them, simply because the engine could not handle more complex actions.

Popular game engines make certain types of actions and behaviors, such as collision and particle detection, easier and more spectacular. Physics engines make the calculation of trajectories easy for activities such as throwing, jumping, or shooting. The ease with which such actions are expressed can sway the designer in certain directions and away from actions more in keeping with other values that a designer might be attempting to express, such as family, community, peace, and sharing. Game engines are often made for first-person shooters. They do not perform as well when serving as venues for other types of content, such as the use of text, slow-moving narratives, deep introspective character dialogue, and believable live-action video.

Illustrative Game: *Quake*

The *Quake* (id Software 1996) engine strongly influenced game design for a decade. It was the first 3D real-time rendering game engine and the first popular networked first-person shooter (figure 3.19).[15] The *Quake* engine worked well due to the way in which the preprocessor reduced the number of shape "faces" by not processing areas of the game level or map that were not visible to the player's point of view. In this way, the environment could be drawn quickly on what now would be considered very slow processors. This technology allowed the presentation of 3D graphics on fairly limited machines.

In *Quake*, the playable character is an unknown protagonist who, in single-player mode, is attacked by monsters, zombies, and other misfortunes during a quest to collect runes and defeat an end boss (the final enemy at the game's conclusion). *Quake* contributed to the process in which game norms from existing two-dimensional games were shifted into 3D spaces, such as "collecting" health in the environment and defeating end bosses. In multiplayer mode, players connect through a server and play either together as one cooperative team or against each other in modes such as death matches. Various player actions—such as collecting grenades, shotgun ammo, and nails for the nailgun—were standardized by the 3D game engine techniques and the institutionalization of prior gameplay shortcuts.

11. Context of Play

The cultures that develop around games affect the playing experience. Such cultures can be found in game worlds such as MMORPGs, in online boards

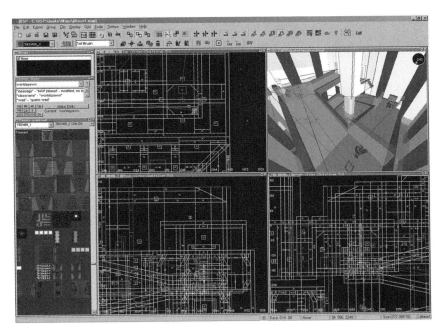

Figure 3.19
The design of the *Quake* engine focused on quick-to-load graphics techniques and a
first-person perspective (id Software 1996).

and player communities, and in the physical environments in which games
are played. Many online multiplayer games provide a relatively hostile environment for new players ("noobs"), who are routinely taunted, exploited,
and attacked by more experienced players. In the opposite vein, *Lord of
the Rings Online* (Turbine, Inc. 2007) celebrates exchanges and generosity.
Game chat occurs in real time and is almost exclusively via voice rather
than text. The game features kinships and other social formations to keep
the bonds between players tight. At any time, players can give to other
players, and the goods involved are created from activities that end up
being quite elaborate. For example, a player can craft cupcakes by finding
ingredients and an oven; these can be exchanged for beer or given freely
out of generosity. The game re-creates the atmosphere and values of J. R. R.
Tolkien's worlds and characters.

Illustrative Game: *Defense of the Ancients 2*
Valve's *Defense of the Ancients* (2003) is a series of real-time session-based
online multiplayer strategy games in which ten players are divided into two

equal teams with the goal of destroying the opposing team's Ancient Structure in their associated stronghold (figure 3.20). Team play and communication are the foundations of the game. Like some online games, it is very "noob unfriendly," meaning that experienced players often treat new players poorly. The hostility of the players who engaged in the first game of the series was well known, and the second game in the series introduced a voice chat feature that furthered hostility. Many players have complained about the unwelcoming, aggressive, and harassing commentary (such behavior directed specifically at female players has been well documented).[16] Voice chat in most cases makes players' gender identity more obvious, which leaves players vulnerable to targeted abuse. Harassment is an ongoing issue within and outside of games. Although there are no reliable statistics on in-game harassment, anecdotal evidence suggests that it is a large problem. In-game harassment also reflects a larger cultural problem: a 2009 study shows that half of U.S. adolescent girls experience sexual harassment (it is often glossed over as "bullying").[17] Blog posts about *Defense of the Ancients* (and other games) are filled with hate speech, and the game's culture is biased against women and players of color. Some people who might otherwise play the game won't do so because of the context of play.[18]

Such problems are not limited to *Defense of the Ancients*. A bullying, unforgiving game culture often challenges new players or those from

Figure 3.20
The context of play for *Defense of the Ancients* is hostile to new players (Valve 2003).

underrepresented groups to "get over it" or get out of the game. A *Battlefield 3* (EA Digital Illusions CE 2011) game launch party in Texas, for example, "disallowed" women from the event to protect them from insults from male players. A statement from organizers is revealing:[19]

Nothing ruins a good LAN party like uncomfortable guests or lots of tension, both of which can result from mixing immature, misogynistic male gamers with female counterparts. Though we've done our best to avoid these situations in years past, we've certainly had our share of problems. As a result, we no longer allow women to attend this event.[20]

That the organizers banned women but welcomed "misogynistic male gamers" says much about the values in this context of play.

12. Rewards

What are points awarded for? What are the game goals? If no points are given, how are players rewarded as they advance in the game? What is the end state of the game? How do you win? The game's reward structure reveals what kinds of accomplishments are valued in the game, and therefore it can be an especially interesting element for values-conscious designers to consider. Aspects of reward systems can include side quests as opposed to mandatory quests, unlockable content, and the requirements for achieving a particular narrative resolution. In *Super Mario Bros.*, for example, the player accumulates a score throughout the game, but many players are motivated by other goals and might regard the score as secondary.

Illustrative Games: *Harpooned* and *SpellTower*

Some activist games expose the values that are laden in common game reward systems by providing ironic rewards. In a game touting itself as prosocial, players might take on the role of a polluting company, for example, and higher scores represent damage caused to the environment. In these cases, higher scores are ironically awarded for behaviors that the game actually opposes. One game with an ironic scoring system is *Harpooned* (Conor O'Kane 2008) (figure 3.21). The game plays in ways that are almost identical to the vertically scrolling "shoot 'em up" arcade games of the early 1980s, like *Galaga* (Namco 1981) and *1942* (Capcom 1984), but the scoring system gives an activist twist to this familiar genre. Players control a Japanese research vessel in Antarctica and are instructed to "perform research on the whales by shooting them with your explosive harpoons." After killing a whale, a player can maneuver the boat toward the whale's remains to collect its meat for "later study." At the end of each level, the meat is offloaded

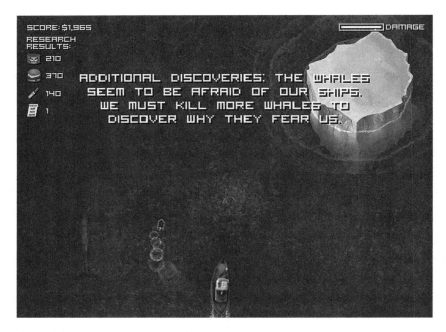

Figure 3.21
Harpooned (Conor O'Kane 2008).

to a "research vessel" where players receive a score that is intended as a sarcastic recognition of their performance. For example, a typical end-of-level score summary tells the player, "Our research has produced 320 cans of pet food, 200 whale burgers, 120 cosmetic products, and 1 scientific paper." Once the scoring system is understood, the game's message becomes clear: the mass slaughter of whales for "research" by Japan is a cover for commercial whaling.

SpellTower (Zach Gage 2011) has a different approach to rewards because the game is not necessarily taking on a social issue (figure 3.22). This seemingly simple casual spelling game incorporates a *Boggle*-style letter mix combined with a *Tetris* stacking game mechanic to allow players to spell words under constraints. The letters are mixed on the screen, and depending on the mode of the game, time-based or turn-based pressure adds to the difficulty. Points are assigned based on the length of the word, and players compete against their own high score.

Rewards in *SpellTower* are carefully designed and deceptively simple. The sounds that are created while combining longer and longer words evolve to develop into a magical indicator of mastery, rewarding the player with

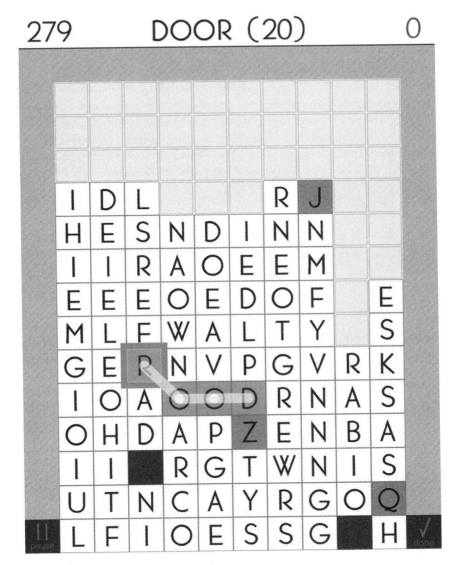

Figure 3.22
SpellTower's sounds and smart glow effects set up a pleasurable encounter with spelling (Zach Gage 2012).

rare sounds for increasing word lengths. Along with the sound design, as the individual letters are constructed into words, they glow and pulse in anticipation of word completion. These small feedback elements make the entering of a high-scoring word extremely rewarding; a completed word explodes from the board, and the letters adjust to the new board state. The highest-scored word is recorded for the player, so players can continually try to best their top word. Often the best words need to be created by working backward and diagonally, and thus the game is set up to reward creative thinking. The final reward—seeing one's best word and the points associated with it—motivates the player for the next round.

13. Strategies

What strategies can be usefully applied in the game? What approaches to the challenges presented in the game will help players progress or win? This element is similar to scoring: strategies can straightforwardly convey values by motivating players to use particular play styles, or they can reward particular play styles for the purpose of ironic critique.

Illustrative Game: *PeaceMaker*
In *PeaceMaker* (ImpactGames 2007), the player inhabits the role of either the Israeli prime minister or the Palestinian president during a particularly volatile period of the Israeli-Palestinian conflict (figure 3.23). Whichever role the player chooses, the goal is to create conditions in which a two-state solution to the conflict becomes viable. There are a wide variety of actions to choose from—some hawkish, some conciliatory, some unilateral, and some that require cooperation with groups on the other side of the conflict.

The game's values can most clearly be discerned by contrasting the types of strategies that lead to success with those that lead to failure. Generally, a hawkish foreign policy will exacerbate the conflict, and small conciliatory gestures will build trust between the two sides. Small gestures set the stage for more significant peace-building policies that can eventually lead to the end of the conflict. The game affirms the value of diplomacy and a nonmilitaristic foreign policy. The player can accept or reject the model's assumptions but is encouraged to consider their applicability to the real-world conflict.

14. Game Maps

Game maps (also called levels or environments) are the custom scenarios—the stages, settings, and mission details—of a game. In most cases, these

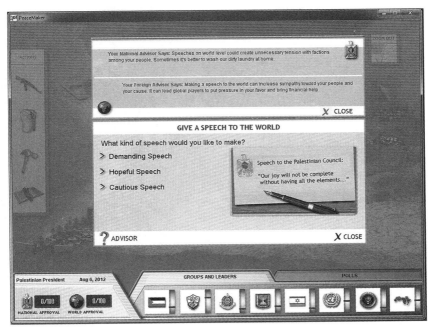

Figure 3.23
Hawk or dove strategies in *PeaceMaker* result in extremely different outcomes and reflect the challenges of a real-world conflict (ImpactGames 2007).

are designed in a grid-based or cubic space. Any spatial arrangement in a game can prioritize particular values. Collaboration, for example, cannot easily happen in confined spaces where teams cannot congregate on screen because players often wish to see the interactions of their friends while fighting together. As another example, generosity might require players to be able to approach or at least recognize other players in the game space or to receive a message from the other players. Thus, both the spatial metaphors alluded to in the design of the game map as well as the actual constraints of the map can foster or prohibit certain values.

Illustrative game: *Left 4 Dead 2*
Left 4 Dead 2 (Valve 2009), the second in a series of zombie games by Valve, is a cooperative first-person shooter set in a postpandemic New Orleans (figure 3.24). The story revolves around four people who are immune to a virulent global disease and who must find other survivors and reach safe havens. Those who are infected become zombies and attack the uninfected.

Figure 3.24
In *Left 4 Dead 2*, the game map is reminiscent of post-Hurricane Katrina New Orleans
(Valve 2009).

The gameplay begins in Savannah, Georgia, and the goal is to reach New Orleans, which is called "The Parish" in the game, a ruined city looking very much as it did in the aftermath of Hurricane Katrina. The game maps shape player experiences with claustrophobic alleys and plenty of confined spaces that provide opportunities for zombie attacks. The fictional Civil Emergency and Defense Agency (CEDA) and the military create safe zones to evacuate as many survivors as possible. Some of the CEDA workers who are wearing hazardous materials (hazmat) suits, however, are already zombies ready to attack.

In the game, the movement of survivors is paramount. In the creation of a virtual New Orleans, the maps needed to use nonlinear spaces to prolong the gameplay, create ambiance, and mirror the variety of spaces found in an older city. Level designer Dario Casali noted that the maps themselves were set by plotting a course that the players (as survivors) would likely travel. For example, the city park that is featured in campaign five is located at the center of the city. With its open spaces bordered by round hedges, this park becomes an ideal place for the designers to situate a "generator," a type of zombie with particular traits (others include "spitter," "charger," and "hunter"). Next in the player's journey is likely the cemetery, a big open space that has crypts, which allows for ambushing and other actions.[21] These open spaces are dangerous and quickly become filled with attackers who create mob scenes that some critics say mirror depictions of New Orleans in crisis after Hurricane Katrina. The game's "director"—the technical artificial intelligence that controls game difficulty—changes the layout of the map as players move through the space. In the cemetery, for example, the layout of crypts is rendered dynamically based on how well a player is doing. The patterns are dynamically generated through game play.[22]

Chet Faliszek, the writer on the project, described the game spaces as the "Deep South," featuring swamps and back roads as well as New Orleans.[23] The space of New Orleans is, to some players and critics, too much for a game to contain after a catastrophe. "Setting the game in a city that was [the] scene of dead, bloated bodies floating by so soon afterward was a bad call," Willie Jefferson of the *Houston Chronicle* wrote in his "Gamehacks" blog. "New Orleans … or the Old South can be very, very touchy areas to deal with."[24] Faliszek comments on the game's depiction of New Orleans: "It's a place we love, it's dear to our hearts. We would not cheapen it. It's not a brick-for-brick representation of New Orleans; it's a fictional version, and I love that city."[25] Yet the spaces that are depicted in the game reveal values that are embedded in level design itself.

On the surface, game maps might appear to have little to do with politics and values. The levels in *Left 4 Dead 2* are computationally generated to adjust to player skill. What can be the politics in those mere creations of location? As we know, Faliszek admits to intentionally evoking the post-Hurricane Katrina setting of New Orleans. But because some game maps are rendered to model this time and place, the game invokes issues in U.S. social history. By creating the rules to render the game map, the designers bring along dimensions of troubled race and socioeconomic disparity that followed in the wake of the disaster. Katrina is not a mere backstory: the game brings with it the tension, the accusations, and representations of those who were most affected. The game is rendering the city dynamically and refers to New Orleans post-Katrina, so race and socioeconomic status seem to be algorithmically embedded in the depiction of the city—a claustrophobic game map filled with desperate zombies.[26]

15. Aesthetics

Although beauty is in the eye of the beholder, the aesthetics of a game express values. All games feature some type of visual look, sonic treatment, or physical movement that links them to the historic concept of aesthetics. Games operate far beyond the functional level: central to any game is its connection to emotion and feeling. Aesthetics impart strong reasons to like or not like a game. They give players the sense of meaning outside and along with the game actions, narrative, and reward. For many players, for example, the *Uncharted* (Naughty Dog 2007) series stands out because it is beautiful and "cinematic." *Uncharted 2* (Naughty Dog 2009) earned much praise for the set pieces in which battle took place, the high degree of visual and aural polish, and its Indiana Jones–style plot. These games differentiate themselves from other action-adventure games in their high production values and cohesive look and feel—in other words, for their aesthetics.

All games have some sort of aesthetic, and many games are beautiful, but the aesthetic moves beyond what is good looking or not and ultimately infuses the game with values. *Journey*, for example, infuses values in several ways. The value of cooperation is integrated through its stunning sound design as the players communicate: the game's beautiful sonic aesthetic emerges from the value of cooperation. The value of curiosity is rewarded by the gorgeous scenes along the quest to the mountain. A game's aesthetics are a primary site of player pleasure and also launch values into play.

Illustrative Game: *Limbo*

The platform game *Limbo* (Microsoft 2010) sets the player in the role of an unnamed boy whose sister has vanished (figure 3.25). The boy can run,

Figure 3.25
The beauty of *Limbo* initially masks some of the cruelty in the game (Playdead 2010).

jump, climb, push, and pull. The game has a strong black-and-white art style, which is especially interesting because the character can momentarily become "lost" in the background and foreground of the world, which consists entirely of shadow shapes. The audio environment is minimal and haunting. Dangerous creatures such as giant spiders emerge from the shadows in a surprising, beautiful, and (for many) horrifying way. The beautiful monochromatic game world has reminded critics of film noir or German expressionist films. The beauty of the game works in contrast to the dark theme and the style of play style that is encouraged. Gruesome animation (dismemberment, beheading) materializes effortlessly and surprisingly from this seemingly simple and otherwise aesthetically stunning world, disrupting feelings of beauty and sympathy with horror. The values of beauty and cruelty emerge together through the play of *Limbo*.

Conclusion

In this chapter, we have examined fifteen categories of game elements—an ontological breakdown of what "makes up" a game. But a couple of warnings are in order. First, meaning emerges not from individual elements but *from the relationships among elements*. This point has been an implicit theme in preceding sections. Recall how point of view and character representation in the *Tomb Raider* games interrelate to cast Lara Croft as an object of voyeuristic pleasure or how *Three Player Chess* introduces supplementary actions and rules to subvert the values of ordinary chess. We see these relationships among elements playing a role that is similar to the syntax of a language, which, along with other systems, enables us to understand how words combine to convey meaning through sentences. Similarly, if we understand the syntax of games, we know how elements combine to convey meaning through play. Second, these elements in any game could plausibly take on a variety of different and even opposing meanings depending on who plays. Values-conscious design and analysis must therefore give full weight to contextual factors, including the variability in players' values, beliefs, and backgrounds.

Groundwork for Values at Play

In these first three chapters, we lay the groundwork for Values at Play. In chapter 1, we establish a theory of values in digital games. In chapter 2, we survey some of the many ways that values can crop up, intentionally or unintentionally, in games. Here in chapter 3, we describe fifteen elements, the raw materials from which the world of a game is built. In the next section of the book, chapters 4 through 7, we take a practical turn. Guided by our theory of values and with the fifteen game elements as our building blocks, we describe the three key components of the Values at Play heuristic—discovery, implementation, and verification—to offer guidance to conscientious designers as they create new games.

II The Values at Play Heuristic

4 Overview of the Heuristic

Designing and building a digital game can be extremely complex, comprising activities with many interwoven layers and dimensions. But more than that, games created for widespread distribution, including commercial distribution, are shaped by input from investors, publishers, executives, designers, and players who desire to direct the multistep process that takes the game from idea to finished product. We are aware that adding values to the equation—a crucial step—increases complexity with a layer that might seem vague and abstract, that is why it is helpful to have a concrete playbook for considering values in design.

The Values at Play (VAP) heuristic is a hands-on, dynamic approach to considering values in design. More concrete than a general command but more open and flexible than a step-by-step method, the VAP heuristic allows progress on a project even when the final goal is not fully articulated. The heuristic can serve as a rough guide for designers who would like to shape the social, ethical, and political values that are embedded in games.[1]

The VAP heuristic includes three components:

Discovery: Discovery involves locating the values that are relevant to a given project and defining those values within the context of the game.
Implementation: Implementation includes translating values into game elements—including specifications, graphics, and lines of code. The heart of design, it is the process of realizing values in terms of the basic practical elements of a game.
Verification: Verification requires establishing the validity of the designer's efforts to discover and implement values. Verification is a form of quality control.

Discovery, implementation, verification: We call these components and not steps because a designer does not first discover values, then implement them, and finally verify. Instead, the process is iterative, just as the software development process is. The word *iterative* means "repeating," and iterative design is a cyclical process of generating ideas, creating prototypes, testing, analyzing, and refining—and then repeating the cycle an indefinite number of times until a desired result is reached or, more pragmatically, until a deadline is reached or funding is depleted. "Software development is definitely an inexact process, which is strongly influenced by the personalities, abilities, and experience of the people doing it. Herein lies much of the problem," the software designer Robert O. Lewis has observed: "No two people given the same problem would ever possibly design and code the same precise software solution, so software is as complicated and varied as the combined cognitive strategies from all the people who contribute to it."[2] What's more, software systems are notoriously filled with bugs,

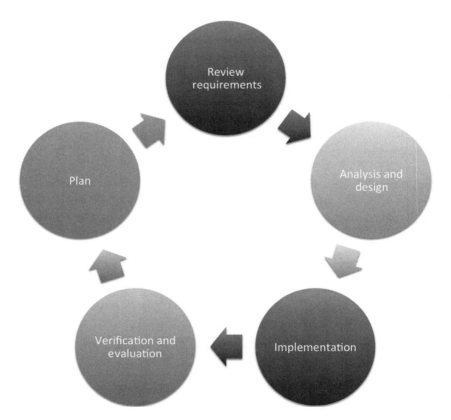

Figure 4.1
A traditional game development cycle.

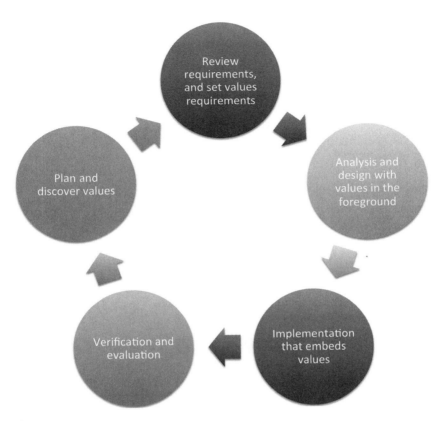

Figure 4.2
The Values at Play development cycle.
Source: This diagram is adapted from Mary Flanagan (2009, 257).

and such bugs have brought down banking systems and postponed space missions. Given all the uncertainties in this process, iterative design serves as quality assurance. The goal of iterative design is to help the technical team move through the development cycle and consistently incorporate feedback from software users—which, in the world of digital games, means players.[3]

The typical development cycle loops in fast turnaround (figure 4.1). "Throughout the entire process of design and development, your game is played," Eric Zimmerman has explained: "You play it. The rest of the development team plays it. Other people in the office play it. People visiting your office play it. You organize groups of testers that match your target audience. You have as many people as possible play the game. In each case, you observe them, ask them questions, and then adjust your design and playtest again."[4] In the case of cascading projects, such as *World of Warcraft* (Blizzard Entertainment 2004), the cycle continues iteratively and also in a cumulative way until the product line closes—often this cycle can be years in the making.

The Values at Play heuristic is iterative, too, but focuses on values during the process of design and building (figure 4.2). In the standard cycle, a developer might ask, did we build the game the customer wanted, and does it respond sensitively to player input? Throughout the VAP cycle, the conscientious designer asks questions, such as, are the values expressed in this game the values that we want to express? Did we implement the values discovered at the onset of the project consistently throughout the game in a meaningful way?

Discovery, implementation, verification: This three-component heuristic helps designers maintain a focus on values, to find expression for those values that they are committed to, and stay alert to observe and eliminate any undesired values that might creep into the game. The next three chapters provide a more detailed account of each of these three components.

5   Discovery

A cancer prevention organization sought out our friend Kris, who has designed many award-winning, innovative games, to see if he might design a mobile game for their charitable organization. A donor to this nongovernmental organization (NGO) felt strongly that the human papillomavirus (HPV) vaccine—a vaccine designed to protect people from the virus, which can cause cervical cancer—was the key for the future of women's health around the world. The donor asked the NGO to push for the vaccine to be distributed in a developing nation, and a country in Africa was chosen as the site for this push. When speaking with Kris, representatives of the NGO started out discussing youth education and focused on the values of well-being, health, equity, access, and empowerment. But when Kris learned that the NGO wanted a mobile game to target eight- to twelve-year-old girls so that they would persuade their parents to help them get vaccinated, he began to question the group's assumptions. Do eight-to twelve-year old girls in this country have mobile phones in order to play a game? How would they be able to sway their parents (often their fathers) to take time from work and travel with them for the vaccination, particularly as it required three shots over three consecutive visits. Kris concluded that the NGO representatives were deeply out of touch with the values and lived experiences of the potential players. Despite the best of intentions, their hopes of changing deeply entrenched cultural values and ways of life with a single game were wildly unrealistic.

Perhaps the worst aspect of this proposal was assessment. When Kris asked the NGO members how they would measure success, they said that they would ask people if they liked the game: "After all, there is no way to measure who is getting a vaccine and who played the game." With criteria for success unconnected to core aims of the game, Kris decided not to engage with the project. The NGO sought a game that would explore an issue, change minds, and even change behavior. But they failed to pursue values discovery in sufficient depth to learn about the cultural expectations and values of the key constituency—its users.

Discovery, as we define it in Values at Play, incorporates two activities: (1) locating values and (2) defining them. The outcome of the first is a set, a list, if you will, of such values as cooperation, peace, fairness, benevolence, tolerance, creativity, liberation, generosity, autonomy, and empathy. Listing, however, is not enough because values as we conceive them for this book, including many with the greatest political, cultural, and historical significance, such as equality, justice, and autonomy, can be abstract, complex, and often ambiguous. Designers need to unravel ambiguity and develop or embrace a definition of relevant values that is sufficiently concrete to guide design—in other words, to be put to work in the context of a game.

The processes of locating and defining values apply to the values that are embodied in the functional description of a game (that is, in the aims of a game) as well as to those that crop up as side effects of myriad other design decisions (call them collateral). Both are revealed in an ongoing process of discovery that starts early in a game's conception and development and continues until all design elements are finally settled.

Locating Values

The VAP heuristic for locating values in a given game project is to consider the diverse influences that shape its values. We suggest four sources as a useful starting place—key actors, functional description, societal input, and technical constraints.

1. *Key actors:* The people involved in creating the game.
2. *Functional description:* The explicit statement describing the game.
3. *Societal input:* Cultural contexts, standards, and other external factors bearing upon the game.
4. *Technical constraints:* The software, hardware, and other game elements that together constitute the game.[1]

1. Key Actors

Games are built by people, for people. Invariably, these people, be they funders, publishers, journalists, players, and designers enter the process through a variety of pathways, explicitly and implicitly.[2] The influences of creators and players may be fairly direct. Funders and publishers who are seeking to serve a global audience may favor values that will increase mass appeal and commercial success. Commercial games, for example, must respond to player expectations of how characters are portrayed and stories are told, which in turn reflect particular palettes of values. When large teams with many layers of management and oversight are involved in the production of a game, all of these people may have a hand in shaping the game's values, whether through explicit intervention or through inadvertent, smaller choices along the way.

The values of designers and individual members of design teams, surprisingly, are often overlooked in this process. Even designers who are not engaged in top-level decisions can have profound effects on a game. The designers' ethnic origins, cultural groups, socioeconomic and political backgrounds, gender identities, education, and disciplinary training shape their perspectives and preferences. These backgrounds can influence which projects they choose to work on as well as the design details they include in their projects.[3]

Keita Takahashi, designer for the 2004 PlayStation game *Katamari Damacy* (Namco 2004) (figure 5.1), noted his individual intentions for the project:

I am influenced by what's going on in reality, and it often shows in what I create. I am sure the terrorist attacks and the war in Iraq, which started just as we began development, affected me in some degree. Of course, I didn't really create this game with a direct reference to the concept of peace, but there are some things that I consciously chose to do here. There is a lot of aggressiveness and violence in games nowadays. I do not denounce this violence completely, because it's a part of human instinct and is a very straightforward thing to express. What I tried to do was not only bring peaceful feelings to the game, but also create something totally different, which would be more exciting than just being peaceful. I wanted to stimulate human instinct on a different level.

Sometimes relevant actors might push in opposing directions. In the case of the development of a Nintendo DS cheerleading game, for example, the lead designer noted that she did not wish to create stereotypically "vapid" cheerleader characters, even though the target audience expected them. When the play testers found that the game veered from their expectations, they rebelled and demanded ditzy cheerleaders. This put players at odds with the members of the design team committed to values of equity, creativity, and so on. Although the design team could not alter the cheerleader theme or aesthetic, they created features to allow players to design uniforms. They also introduced a fashion competition: players who perform well earn other team's uniforms when they beat them. The designers hoped that adding to the game's complexity would make the surface stereotypes less central to the play experience and foster creativity as a value.[4]

Figure 5.1
A street scene from *Katamari Damacy* (Namco 2004).

Experience with the cheerleading game reveals the influence of another key constituency in values—players. As revealed in surveys, informal feedback, and systematic study, players' preferences may shape design in ways that are relevant to values. The market performance of completed products also constitutes an important, although less direct, index of users' values. User-driven innovations (particularly in open-source contexts and in user-generated content such as add-ons and Facebook games) can drastically change the values expressed in games. With the rise of the iterative design process and participatory approaches, designers and developers seek to incorporate feedback from users early in the design and development process.

The push and pull of the preferences and values of diverse constituencies was a significant factor in the development of Mary Flanagan's *The Adventures of Josie True* (2000), the first online adventure game for girls (figure 5.2). Flanagan and her student team drew over forty character portraits, some of which were nearly identical to Barbie and other well-known female characters. The portraits were then shown to middle-school girls. When girls were asked, "Which of these characters might be the heroine of a new game?," they overwhelmingly chose drawings resembling Barbie. But when asked, "Which might become a friend of yours?," the girls overwhelmingly chose the character who ultimately became Josie True. At this juncture, the conscientious designer has a choice—to stay close to predictable, existing

Figure 5.2
Josie, from *The Adventures of Josie True* (Mary Flanagan 2000).

commercial expectations or to risk a new look, style, attitude, or behavior for a character. The designer chose the latter to fight stereotypes and promote the values of equity and fairness of representation. Players of the finished game commented positively on the character.[5]

The longer a game has been been in use the greater the opportunity for designers to use iterative design cycles to adapt to users' values and preferences.[6] Nowhere has this been better in evidence than in Blizzard's *World of Warcraft* (2004). In early versions of the game, players were allowed to select their character within specific parameters. They selected a character belonging to a faction and a race, with each race possessing characteristic strengths and limitations. An Alliance Gnome, for example, could be a Warrior or a Warlock but not a Priest. Players had to choose their character's class and race combination wisely because these factors could benefit or hinder game play. Responding to an onslaught of player petitions, however, Blizzard changed these constraints to allow for more flexible character combinations. These were primarily visual rather than instrumental—a choice about aesthetics, not functionality. Further, by changing the financial models for character selection, Blizzard allows players to pay extra to alter a character's

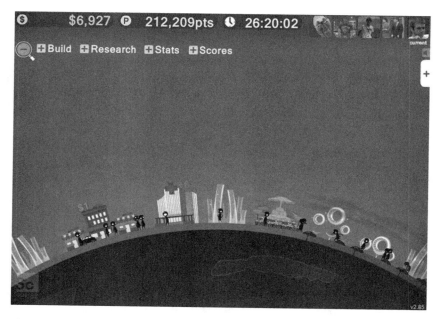

Figure 5.3
A miniature planet, from *Power Planets* (Area/Code 2010).

race midgame. Players also can pay extra to have their characters change factions from Horde to Alliance or vice versa. These changes in the game have, interestingly, been a source of extra revenue, while providing players greater latitude to express their preferences and values.

This chapter's sidebar (at the end of the chapter), written by designer Frank Lantz, is an incisive account of how he and members of his company, Area/Code, handled some value questions in their 2010 Facebook game, *Power Planets* (figure 5.3). Designed for the Discovery Channel, the game promoted a television series about alternative energy. The design team was committed to the big-picture question: "What values are at play in the subject of mankind's energy consumption?" By focusing on the complex issues of how humans consume energy, they were able to shape specific design decisions along the way. Lantz's account is an informative tale of values discovery.

A final example of value discovery comes from Flanagan's recent series of games addressing biases and stereotypes, particularly around barriers to women in science, for the National Science Foundation. Flanagan and her team at Tiltfactor prototyped several games, such as *Awkward Moment* (Mary Flanagan 2012a) (figure 5.4), that use novel strategies to reduce bias.

Figure 5.4
Awkward Moment, a game that helps reduce bias (Mary Flanagan 2012a).

In this case, key actors were designers, on the one hand, and, on the other, funders (scientists and government officials). Although, initially, the unexpected approach taken by designers was surprising to the funders, testing data persuaded them of the game's efficacy. The game *Buffalo: The Name Dropping Game* (Mary Flanagan 2012b) (figure 5.5) prompted a similar skepticism, later overcome. These experiences reveal the important tug and pull generated by varying perspectives of diverse key actors.

Because there is a wide diversity of key actors whose desires, preferences, and values shape a game, differences and conflicts almost certainly will arise and will pull the design in diverse directions. In the microcosm of creating games, designers confront a plurality of values. Should designers' inclinations win out over the audience in this tug of war with values? Is giving players exactly what they expect or want a good idea? Should it matter that player desires are shaped by marketing materials, prior games, and the dominant culture? Should the designer's values trump the values of the marketplace, or vice versa? These and other similar questions of responsibility are often neglected in the moment-to-moment decisions that shape game creation. Although we do not have general answers, we are certain that these questions should be asked. Specific responses depend on specific features of those cases (such as the nature of the game, its audience,

Figure 5.5
Buffalo, a game that highlights feelings of injustice (Mary Flanagan 2012b).

its context, and so forth) and on the nature of other sources of values, to which we now turn.

2. Functional Description

Imagine you visit a website and read the description of a game, or see an advertisement for it. Or, perhaps you are part of a design group, articulating the early goals and ideas. At these moments, you will find formulations of a game's functional description. Typically written at the start of a game development project, the functional description may or may not refer to values. When it does, it offers a top-level guide to values that the game developers intend to express.[7] This is what we mean when we identify functional description as one of the key sources of values at play in a game.

As a designer, you may be creating a game with a particular value in mind. You may be interested in changing people's perspectives, calling them to action, or motivating them to advocacy. Your game may be designed to cue people's attention to environmental conservation, to stir empathy for the victims of war, or to inflame their indignation over racial, cultural, religious, or gender biases. You may be seeking to deepen their understanding of complex social issues, such as strife in a certain region, natural disasters, or global warming. On a more personal scale, you may be interested in a game that explores friendship, cooperation, solidarity, generosity, love, or security or one that stimulates creativity, joy, tolerance, liberation, autonomy, or independence. If any of these is one of the primary aims of your game, you are likely to express them through its functional definition.

Functional descriptions of games can include values, but they also feature prominently in general technology design. Although values like accessibility and fairness may draw the attention of designers as they develop or critique educational software and search engines, they also are incorporated into the very DNA of a system when they are aspects of its functional description. Thus, when designers set out to develop fair search engines or accessible educational systems for the disabled, values explicitly drive and define a system's shape. Privacy, for, example, has inspired a growing host of "privacy-enhancing tools" for Web browsing, email, social media, and more. The expression of values in functional definition is evident in many games.

The Web-based game *Darfur Is Dying* (Susana Ruiz 2005) was created by a student team from the University of Southern California and published by mtvU (figure 5.6). The goal of the project was (1) to raise awareness of the humanitarian crisis in the Darfur region of western Sudan, which was caused by a conflict between Sudanese government troops and non-Arabic

Figure 5.6
A scene from *Darfur Is Dying* (Susana Ruiz 2005).

militias, and (2) to generate a grassroots movement among college students in the United States and other Western nations to end the conflict through government intervention. By positioning players as refugees, the game aimed to stir empathy, provoke engagement with the crisis, stimulate efforts to provide basic survival goods, restore community, and establish democracy and freedom.

Quest Atlantis (Sasha Barab et al. 2005), a game that was developed by Sasha Barab and his research team at the University of Indiana, engaged children ages nine to twelve in dramatic play involving both online and real-world learning activities. Primarily focusing on game quests, the project's definition is a rich source of values:

QA combines strategies used in the commercial gaming environment with lessons from educational research on learning and motivation. Participation in this game is designed to enhance the lives of children while helping them grow into knowledgeable, responsible, and empathetic adults. [8]

The website for *Quest Atlantis* also includes a discussion of the project's commitment to values:

The QA project will foster an awareness of seven critical dimensions in order to actualize them in the lives of children:

- Creative Expression—"I Create"
- Diversity Affirmation—"Everyone Matters"
- Personal Agency—"I Have Voice"
- Social Responsibility—"We Can Make a Difference"
- Environmental Awareness—"Think Globally, Act Locally"
- Healthy Communities—"Live, Love, Grow"
- Compassionate Wisdom—"Be Kind"[9]

The functional descriptions of both *Darfur Is Dying* and *Quest Atlantis* disclose key goals of the project and include explicit commitments to values.

3. Societal Input

The range of values that individuals bring to technical projects is constituted partially (some would say entirely) by society. Yet despite the coconstituency of individuals with societies, collective and institutional societal sources of values are influential and worthy of special note.

Even a simple kitchen appliance that toasts bread must meet societal standards: its plug must fit into a wall socket, and it should not catch fire or short out the electrical system. Information systems and infrastructures (such as Web browsers, network switches, and email systems) should meet standards of robustness, security, and confidentiality. Other performance standards—energy efficiency for appliances, gas mileage for vehicles, emission limits on industrial machines—reflect societal expectations. With video games, industry ratings warn parents of the presence of explicit sexual content, foul language, violence, and other "mature" content, and these warnings may shape games as designers strive to meet or avoid particular ratings. Whether the intent is a commitment to "good, clean fun" or simply to sell more games, the result is a media product shaped by societal standards that are embodied in these ratings' schemes.

As a source of values, societal input can be deeply politically charged. In the 1990s, a U.S. state department of education objected to an educational game about American history that included gay rights activism. Although the designer (coauthor Flanagan) was inspired by values of equity, inclusion, and fairness, the education department threatened to forbid schools from purchasing the game if it included information on gay rights activism, and the publisher required the designer to remove these parts before it would release the game. In this way, societal mores became a source of values in the design of the game through the direct intervention of the publisher (through its desire to presumably increase sales) and the indirect intervention of the state authority (through its mandates). The mechanisms of influence can vary significantly—from explicit demand (as in this case) to the indirect, sometimes subtle influences of cultural and historical contexts.

4. Technical Constraints

Beyond societal standards, functional definition, and key actors, the technologies on which games are layered impose their own constraints and affordances. Creators of games face a multitude of major and minor decisions during the design and development phases, and these decisions may have implications for values. Some emerge as a result of explicit design choices, and others emerge inadvertently as designers focus on producing some other effect. As noted in the discussion of game elements in chapter 3, almost every aspect of a game can be freighted with values, offering both opportunities and dangers to those at the design helm. We like the term *collateral* for these values because although they do not steer a project from the outset, as do those in a functional description, they appear along the way to an astute designer, often as a result of technical limitations and affordances, as significant side constraints.

Values that emerge from technical decisions are common in nongame contexts, too. Interface developers who use visual cues inadvertently discriminate against visually impaired users, thereby undermining the value of inclusiveness. Location-based services, which are now common on mobile devices, can allow third-party surveillance of individuals, a potential violation of privacy. Some search engines prioritize results according to advertising fees, impinging on transparency and fairness. In each of these cases, designers may have focused on efficiency or utility, and they may have been working around limitations of screen size, performance, bandwidth, formalism, and a myriad others. But their decisions, whether intentional or forced, have consequences in the realm of values.[10]

The same is true in games. A driving simulation game may not specify any particular values among its aims, but designers nonetheless must make decisions about car models, car colors, driver avatars, player point of view, obstacles in the car's path, and more. As these decisions accumulate, the designers may find a culture emerging that expresses a set of values in their design choices.[11] This is an example of the "collateral" values that are mentioned in the introduction to this chapter: sometimes values appear in games not intentionally but as a result of other design decisions. In deciding a game's storyline, resolution, and arc—as well as game goals, scoring, and available actions—a designer may contribute to a player's experience of embodied values.

Consider the introduction of Real ID, a feature on the online gaming service Battle.net. With Real ID, game players' friends appear under their real-life names on a "friends" list, alongside whatever characters they are playing on any of the Battle.net games (figure 5.7). Players see their friends' real names when communicating in-game, chatting, or viewing their character's profile. Players do not have to recall which friend is playing under what character on what server.

Previously, players could chat or perform certain game actions (such as running dungeons) only with others on the same server. But with Real ID, they can chat and run a dungeon with those on other servers. Previously, raids in *World of Warcraft* were server-specific. Now, a battle group is a collection of servers, and instances belong to that battle group. Before Real ID, the collection of players was anonymous because players controlled a variety of characters with different names. With Real ID, players may group with their friends instead of inheriting strangers in a raid group. The active community of the server ran its own forums and battles, so the expansion from local to global has affected the personal connections expressed in play. The aim of Real ID was to open up friendship and community outside the technological paradigm of the server-based community. But this technical decision had other effects. There was a loss of anonymity and privacy, a loss of loyalty to one's own server community, and a loss of

Figure 5.7
Many guilds are created among friends. Here are a group of one of the author's
friends in their guild *Varsity Cheer Squad*.

sociality as mixing with strangers in a group declined. Such are the collateral results that designers must be aware of when dealing with the technical
constraints of gaming systems.

Other technical constraints support values whether the designer knows
about it or not. Flanagan's Tiltfactor Laboratory conducted a study on
learning about disease spread and systems thinking through a game that
was implemented nearly identically as a board game and an iPad game.
In randomized controlled experiments, the researchers found that players
played the game 10 to 20 percent faster on the iPad and spoke to each other
10 to 20 percent less during turn-based play, even though conditions for
play among the play sessions were identical. This study showed the design
team that some affordances are particular to each medium and need far
more study.

Defining Values

Thus far, we have answered the question "What values are at play in this
design project?" by focusing on locating values. But answering the discovery question also involves defining these values, not necessarily to provide
a universal analysis of relevant values but to develop a clear and consistent
meaning. Ethical and political values (such as justice, fairness, privacy, tolerance, autonomy, and liberty) are conceptually abstract, controversial, and

notoriously difficult to define. Yet when we reach for them to describe a political system, a relationship, an organization, or a competition, we have in mind definitions or interpretations that are concrete, specific, and operational. Transforming a value from an abstraction to a fully articulated concept makes it accessible to design and capable of influencing architecture and features. It is the work of definition and analysis that forms a necessary bridge between abstract value concepts and concretely articulated conceptualizations able to guide a designer's hand.

Defining values in operational terms is more than employment for idle philosophers. If values are carelessly or inaccurately defined, if those involved have very different understandings, or if the substantive nature of the value is incorrectly construed, then even a beautifully designed, well-executed system can miss its mark. In many instances, implementation—the translation in design from idea to feature (discussed in the next chapter)—may take place implicitly and without much ado. With controversial values, however, good intentions and technical competence may not be enough. The designer also must be guided by a sound and reflective grasp of the value concept.

Consider some examples from nongaming technology. Imagine you are designing a digital repository of medical records and are concerned to protect privacy. How you define it—whether as patient control over information or as appropriateness of information flow[12]—will make a difference in how you design your repository. Or consider openness, a value that has been controversial among software designers, especially those within the free and open-source communities. Does an open system mean that anything goes, or can a system be considered open even if some constraints are placed on how it can be developed? Similarly, can an open network place constraints on those who join or connect, or can they place requirements of protocol or good behavior? Well-defined concepts (privacy, openness, or any other value at play) are of more than philosophical interest: they have genuine consequences for the technologies in our lives.

In the game world, you might be interested in promoting generosity. How should this value be understood? In some massively multiplayer online role-playing games (MMORPGs), players who have acquired more powerful resources give their older, less useful items to lower classes of players. This sharing is not required by the game, and typically there is no explicit reward for gifting the items. As in real life, however, sharing goods and objects can incur social benefits, such as loyalty and increased reputation. Players value these kinds of social rewards, and thus some form of generosity has become common. But what if generosity is rewarded by the system?

In *Asheron's Call* (Turbine 1999), in-game "mentors" keep a percentage of the experience points earned by their mentees. If generosity is rewarded in a game, is it really generosity? Do material rewards eliminate the possibility of genuinely generous play? And if there are no explicit rewards for generosity, does this encourage players to focus on social rewards, such as friendship or teamwork? On the other hand, if experience points or other reward systems are used to encourage generosity, how does this influence relationships between mentors and mentees? Does generosity require that you give something to someone else or that the thing you give is something of value? Does it require that the giving *hurt* or diminish the stock of the giver? Or must it merely increase the stock of the receiver?[13] Such questions must be answered by the team to define the value adequately.

Cooperation requires that people work together toward a common end. But must the work together be fully voluntary, or is it still cooperation if coercion is involved? How does one define loyalty? Does it call for unfair favoritism or merely a commitment to the good of another when all else is equal? Crucial to this exploration are the site-specific negotiation and definition of these values. The range of interpretation available to both the designer and the player is vast.

The research project RAPUNSEL (2003–2006), undertaken by coauthor Flanagan and her colleagues at New York University and funded by the National Science Foundation, was intended to teach basic computer science to girls from low-income backgrounds.[14] The designers, in other words, sought to promote social justice through gender equity. These broad, abstract values could be made real through improved mastery over a high-status skill. Before they could design the game, however, the team needed to discover the values at play (justice, equity) and also define them. Their goals depended on several key philosophical and empirical propositions. One is the prominent role of information technologies in contemporary Western societies. Another is the importance of proficiency in quantitative and analytic skills as a source of social and cultural status, including high-paying jobs. "Programming is the most powerful medium of developing the sophisticated and rigorous thinking needed for mathematics, for grammar, for physics, for statistics, and all the 'hard' subjects," Seymour Papert has asserted: "I believe more than ever that programming should be a key part of the intellectual development of people growing up."[15] Studies of women, however, have unequivocally revealed low interest and achievement in these areas by at least early adolescence. As a result, women have limited access to many well-paid, high-status jobs.[16] RAPUNSEL researchers designed a game to function as a learning environment for computer programming that would appeal to middle-school girls. Its aim was to intervene in a dominant pattern of inequitable distribution and access of goods. Accordingly, justice and equality were defined operationally for the RAPUNSEL project game, *Peeps* (RAPUNSEL 2006), in terms of increasing and access to higher-paying, higher-status professional employment.

Discovery for Designers

Designers and other stakeholders shape games in ways that are relevant to values. Players also bring values and expectations to a game, shaping them directly through feedback and play, and indirectly through the marketplace. Societal factors generate background expectations, and technical constraints and affordances yield outcomes with values' dimensions. Prior to any of these, values may be (though need not be) expressed in the very conception of a game through its functional definition.

The work of discovery is specifying, seeking, finding, understanding, conceptualizing, articulating, and defining values that are relevant to your game. It may take place at any time during design—before it begins, through completion, and even beyond as values emerge in play itself. The discovery component makes conscientious designers astute and systematic in their awareness of values at play. It is the necessary foundation for our active engagement with them.

The Power of Values

by Frank Lantz, Creative Director and Cofounder, Area/Code, Zynga New York

In 2010, Area/Code developed a Facebook game called *Power Planets* for the Discovery Channel. The game's goal was to promote a TV series about alternative energy sources called *Powering the Future*. The experiences that we had while creating this game may serve as a useful example of how thinking about values influences the game design process on multiple levels.

Let's start with the values that were involved in our taking on this project in the first place. *Power Planets* is a work-for-hire game development project. Its raison d'être is to drive awareness of and interest in a television series. It is, in a word, advergaming, and that's not a pretty word. Many of Area/Code's projects were games of this type. How did we reconcile our game design values (a desire to make meaningful, high-quality, innovative games) with the vulgar demands of consumerist propaganda? To be honest, we did not have to try hard. We had found that this context for creating games provided a surprising amount of creative freedom. Our interests were primarily formal, and our main passion was game systems and structures. The requirement to express the themes of some existing media entity was a kind of arbitrary constraint that we actually found quite useful. Moreover, there is a certain amount of ambiguity about what makes a successful game of this type. More often than not, the creative goal of making a good, original, and interesting game lined up closely enough with our clients' strategic goals.

But we did take seriously the obligation to explore the themes that we were given. In the case of *Power Planets*, the TV show that it promoted had not yet been created, so we had only an outline of the subjects that it would explore. This was essentially a broad overview of the challenges related to energy consumption over the next few hundred years.

What values are at play in the subject of energy consumption? We use energy to improve our lives, to achieve our goals, to satisfy our preferences. There are different kinds of energy, each with its own costs and benefits. Some of these costs take the form of negative externalities: burdens like pollution are shared by a community beyond those getting the direct benefit of the energy consumption. Sometimes these burdens are distributed not geographically but across time: future generations will shoulder some of the costs of current energy consumption.

The design team spent time researching and discussing these issues. Each member of the team brought his or her own opinions to the mix, but eventually we came to the conclusion that this issue is contentious because it's genuinely complex. None of us felt there were easy truths that a game about energy should embody or express.

Like many contentious issues, energy policy mixes together math problems and values problems. By math problems, I mean empirical questions, questions of fact, engineering problems. Math problems alone can be difficult. We can disagree about matters of fact ("How much oil is left?"). We can disagree about the proper way to frame the problem ("How far in advance of running out of oil should we begin transitioning away from using it?"). We can disagree about the best type of solutions to pursue ("Should we focus on using oil more efficiently or on finding better ways to replace it?"). In general, however, we understand how to approach math problems. We know the kind of criteria to use for measuring success and the type of tradeoffs that we will have to make to get there. We want to maximize our benefits and minimize our costs. Once we're in the realm of numbers, there's no need for the kind or ferociously emotional dispute that surrounds energy use and environmental impact.

But before we can enter the realm of numbers, we have to agree on far more nebulous matters: What constitutes a benefit, and what constitutes a cost? Which benefits are better than others, which costs are worse, and by how much? This is the realm of values. How much is unspoiled wilderness worth? How costly is diminished biodiversity? What exactly is our moral obligation to our neighbors, to our future selves, and to our children's children? These questions cannot be answered in technical terms, yet math questions and values questions have become messily entangled in the public discourse on energy usage.

Games, too, often merge these kinds of problems together. Often they do so on purpose, as when a single-player game makes the player choose between doing something to achieve the game's explicit goal and doing something that seems morally better within the game's story (for examples, see every triple-A game made in the past ten years).

Luckily, we weren't making a single-player game. We were making a Facebook game, and we decided to use the formal qualities of this platform to pry apart these two kinds of problems. The goal was to make a game whose mechanical center was a big, well-defined math problem and whose value problem resided entirely in the social domain in the relationships between the players.

Specifically, we decided to focus on what we considered one of this issue's biggest and most interesting value problems—our moral responsibility to the future. Much of the difficulty of energy issues involves thinking through consequences on a planetary time scale. It's hard to determine what moral weight we should give to the preferences of the people who will live long after we've died. After all, it's hard enough for humans to figure out the proper weight to give our own future preferences. That's why we drink too much, overeat, procrastinate, and avoid exercise. Attempting to delineate our responsibility to future generations is like multiplying that problem by many orders of magnitude. Intuitively, we feel that there is some responsibility. When the future generation is our own children, our feeling of responsibility is enormous. But when the future generations are more distant or not directly related to us, that feeling is more tenuous. We feel it is right to sacrifice some of our own goals and desires to benefit these future people, but how much? And what if we frame this relationship as one of harm instead of benefits? At what point do our rights directly impinge on theirs? No discussion of energy policy and environmental impact can happen without considering these questions, but they are questions that our brains find difficult to contemplate, much less answer.

Power Planets used the power of gaming to explore this issue. In the game, the player manages a small, simulated planet, earning points by building and powering structures that serve the needs and wants of inhabitants. But players are in control of their planet for only a limited amount of time because every few days the game switches planets between players: everyone's current planet is given to someone else to manage. After five hand-offs (called "epochs"), a planet was retired. The planet-management simulation itself is filled with complex tradeoffs that reflect the challenges of energy strategy. Different types of energy production had different levels of effect on the planet's environment, which in turn affected the efficiency of the point-producing structures you built. Oil and coal were cheap and powerful but finite and highly polluting. Alternative power sources, like wind and solar, were limitless and clean but required expensive research and were less efficient overall.

Every planet you managed was like a little puzzle involving limited resources and overlapping constraints. You had to make complex decisions about what types of structures and power systems to build and when and how to transition from one type of power to another. *Power Planets*, however, was about more than just the moment-to-moment tradeoffs you encountered in managing the simulation. We wanted the real focus of the game experience to be the tension between the immediate impact of your decisions and their long-term consequences. How would your decisions affect the players who inherited your planet "downstream"?

Our goal was to have the player constantly feel the desire to squeeze as many points as possible out of the planet under their control and then to consider how that would affect the next player down the line. We wanted players to experience gratitude when they received a planet whose previous owner had kept it in great shape, rationing scarce resources and investing in long-term research. And we wanted players to experience the pain of receiving a planet whose previous owner had turned it into a smog-choked, strip-mined wasteland.

During the design process, we struggled with the question of how to express the tension between the explicit goal of maximizing points and the implicit goal of cooperating with other players. Should we have two different kinds of points or a reputation system that allowed players to rate each other? Ultimately, we decided that the best option was the simplest: the goal of the game was to score the most points, and the leader board tracked each player's average score per planet. This encouraged players to get the most points they could out of every planet they managed. Any negative consequences for sticking their friends with a hopelessly ruined planet would be felt purely in the social realm and in their conscience.

There was, however, a second leader board for planets. This board ranked each completed planet by the total points that it produced over its lifespan, along with the five players who had managed it. The juxtaposition of the two leader boards highlighted the tension between the two ways of approaching the game. You could play selfishly, without considering the effect that your actions would have on other players, or you could play altruistically, balancing your own gain with some consideration for others. There was no way you could be on top of both leader boards.

In fact, getting onto the planet leader board required a certain kind of faith. To maximize the overall point gain across five separate epochs, players needed to use the limited resources under their control to set up situations that would pay off long after their epoch was over. They compromised their own profit to ensure that future players would survive and prosper. Who inherited a planet, however, was beyond the players' control. If the next player was selfish or stupid or both, then your sacrifice was in vain. The winning planets would be those lucky enough to string together five players who had each decided to take this leap of faith. Looked at in this way, you could see the choice to play altruistically not as a rejection of the game's math problem, but as an attempt to solve a larger, subtler math problem, one that required a mastery of the game's mechanical systems, collaboration with distant, silent partners, cleverness, empathy, luck, and trust.

There was no "correct" way to play *Power Planets*, no right or wrong choices, no message that we wanted to transmit about the proper way to manage our energy needs and limited resources. We wanted to create a game in which the elusive qualities of these issues were highlighted, the small details magnified, the vast incomprehensible scale of the problem compressed into something that could be considered and passed on to a friend.

For us, this was the ultimate lesson about values at play that we learned from the process of creating *Power Planets*. Games can explore the complicated and ambiguous world of values because they are dynamic models, simulations, and imaginary spaces and also because they function as stylized forms of social interaction. Games are a way for people to engage with issues through the entanglement between a dynamic system and the aspects of the world that it points to and reflects, as well as through the entanglement between those things, ourselves, and each other.

6 Implementation

Sally, a veteran game designer and writer, finished the script for a sequel to a role-playing game for children. The first game featured a strong female protagonist who had a geeky male sidekick, and for the sequel, the brand owners wanted to shift hero characters among the cast. In her script for the second game, Sally created a new male lead, a female sidekick, and a stereotypical evil scientist as a villain. Everyone on the extended team approved the script, but when two marketing people ("outsiders") finally read the finished script, they felt that the sidekick came off as a histrionic worrywart who was completely dependent on the male hero character. Her lack of agency was reinforced by other characters, such as the domineering villain, who treated her in a patronizing, sexist manner. She was bullied and embarrassingly stereotypical. Although the geeky male sidekick of the first game also did not really have agency, his character did not conform to a gender stereotypes in the same way as did the female counterpart.

Sally had to address their concerns. "I had a knee-jerk reaction," Sally admits. "I was angry. I'm a woman designer, and the team counted on me to have that perspective. Of course I'm going to treat women fairly in my writing! Who do these outside people think they are? Do they have nothing better to do than to harass me? But this question of agency showed me that no one is perfect, especially when referencing game roles." Sally went on to reflect that the incident was vital to making a better, more equitable game. "This was a bit of conventional wisdom turned on its head—'Don't let marketing see it yet'—because in this case, the marketing people were women who had a perspective that was missing from other parts of the team, and I could have actually used their eyes on the problem earlier."

The problem arose partly because of the need to differentiate the second game's characters from those in the first game and partly because of a failure to notice some stereotypical characterizations, which Sally later admitted "In the end, it is really useful to have a second pair of eyes and reflective processes in order to help writers and designers hit the mark. We don't have to be afraid of making mistakes because it will reflect on our credentials as good people. And this is everyone's job, and why working in teams is good, and why diverse teams matter."

Once the problem was noted and acknowledged it was relatively easy to fix. Sally spent a day adjusting the character and improving interactions among nonplayer characters. She is convinced that the game is now much better: "I was not looking at how all the parts fit into the whole. Problems emerge, particularly when using a familiar form, because the structure is familiar and old structures bring along some dated inequities that you have to watch out for.... In the discovery and ideation process, it is difficult to see these problems emerging. The development of general characters and sidekicks sounds innocuous from a 50,000-foot view. There has to be a conscious effort to watch for conflicts in values as the details of implementation emerge. Sometimes you personally can have very strong values, yet still you might resort to caricature and stereotypes. Values at Play offers a way to put a check on your process. This systematic check is a way to avoid unintentional biases from creeping in."

Values for a given project must be translated into specifications for graphics, scripts, and lines of code. This process is what we call *implementation*—the transformation of a creative vision, ideas, aspirations, and fundamental requirements into a playable artifact. Implementation is the heart of game creation and design.

This chapter addresses the question that a conscientious designer might ask: how can I pursue a great game and still think about values? The question itself sounds ambiguous, a bit like asking how one bakes bread. One way of answering is to provide a recipe: add one teaspoon of salt to five cups all-purpose flour; stir a packet of dry yeast into a half cup of warm water and wait ten to fifteen minutes until the mixture is foamy; and so on. Another way of answering is to provide a set of principles: identify various bread-baking paradigms, and explain the properties of key ingredients (such as flour types, raising agents, and sweeteners) and the ways that each contributes to the baking enterprise. The first answer is more likely to result in an immediate product; the second develops the skill and know-how of the baker. Designing with values in mind, like design in general, draws on art, science, and practical wisdom. Implementing values in a specific game engages knowledge, experience, intuition, creativity, and testing within an iterative cycle of discovery, trial, and improvement. It calls for a focus on the artifact and the diverse factors in its context of use. Accordingly, implementation does not lend itself to a step-by-step recipe. Instead, revealing guiding principles through cases offers greater flexibility and adaptability that is better suited to the challenges that a designer might face.

In this chapter, we illustrate implementation with several cases that are drawn from our own experiences as well as those of others. Although creative inspiration is an essential part of the practice, two heuristic devices provide supplemental stepping stones:

1. *Pay systematic attention to a game's elements.* In this process, designers consider the full range of a game's elements, such as narrative, character representation, game actions, and even the substrate of game engines and hardware. This opens a wide array of ways to implement a given value. Although successful implementation is often a challenge, designers may improve their odds by creatively but systematically seeking different combinations and striking out in unusual directions. The VAP heuristic does not require adoption of the specific analysis of games elements that we offer in this book. The key idea is to conceive of all analytic components (under whatever analysis one prefers) as potential vehicles for values implementation.

2. *Consider what you are trying to achieve and how your game conveys values to players (and potentially others).* You might be interested in changing behavior (for example, through generous deeds), enabling a valued performance (through creativity), inducing a desired experience (freedom or its opposite, for example), or inducing feelings (such as empathy, disgust, or shame) to attune players to certain issues and affect their inclinations to act. With values such as peace, racial justice, and democracy, you may aim for a cognitive effect (to engage users' beliefs, prejudices, and emotions or deepen their understanding and appreciation of issues). Because players may not experience a game in the ways a designer intends, an iterative design process that includes values in a play-testing regimen is essential for the implementation process.[1]

Translation: Practice and Process

Among games that aim to shape beliefs, understanding, and preferences, *Homefront* (Kaos Studios 2011) is one example from the AAA ("triple A") world of high-quality games developed for major platforms with high marketing budgets. Lead level designer Rex Dickson has revealed that his team's aim was to create a "feeling of sympathy for the plight of innocents caught in war. There are universal themes in our game that all humans react to on a very visceral level—babies and children caught in the crossfire, or a home stolen and turned into a prison. A loss of your identity under a brutal occupation."[2] In the discovery phase, designers noted that the game needed to have a balance between player agency (manifesting the value of freedom) and investment in the narrative. This was crucial to the values that the designers wanted to express. For designer Chris Cross, in first-person shooters, players cannot see themselves and thus have no one to identify with—no mirror that reveals how the character's actions would be received socially. But he did not want to give up the familiar shooter mechanic: if players already knew the key actions and did not need to learn a new mechanic, then they could be more fully immersed in the narrative of the game. So the team designed three allies who would accompany the player character, express human reactions to game situations, and foster empathy.[3] They focused on character, player choice, and rules for interaction with nonplayable characters as elements that help create meaningful experiences and support the core values of empathy. Although the game stays within the familiar conventions of the first-person shooter, it achieves a complex, values-rich design goal.

Finally, as hard as conscientious designers may work to implement values in games, values that are at play are as much a function of the circumstances in which a game is played as the contours of the game itself. By considering the interaction of features with the context of play, designers might discover ways to take advantage of this interplay to achieve their goals even more effectively.

Case: *Pipe Trouble*

In *Pipe Trouble* (Pop Sandbox 2012), values are in evidence in many of the game's elements, including narrative premise and goals, player actions, player choices, rules for interaction with nonplayable characters, rules for interaction with the environment, and rewards. Socially responsible "games for impact" highlight these elements while addressing pressing social and political issues. *Pipe Trouble* was funded by Canada's public broadcaster TVO and developed in conjunction with the film *Trouble in the Peace* (Pinder 2012). In this game, players lay natural gas pipelines in Canada under constraints to make a profit and move natural gas from the beginning to the end of the level. The game uses a rerelease of the classic *Pipe Mania / Pipe Dream* (Lucasfilm 1989), where players construct a connected pipe over a long distance to generate conversations about the environmental effects of natural gas pipelines. Like many games, *Pipe Trouble* uses a familiar mechanic and over-the-top scenarios to engage players. It uses critiques from vandals, politicians, and the media as in-game penalties emerging from the community.

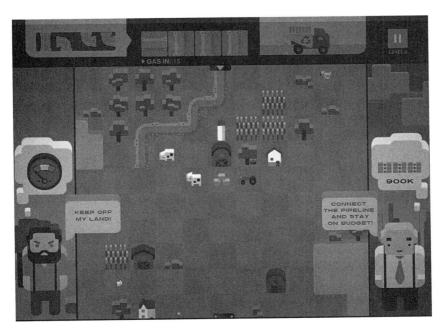

Figure 6.1
Troubling community issues, from *Pipe Trouble* (Pop Sandbox 2012).

The narrative that emerges in this game is one of cleverness in handling local protests, and the values that emerge are self-interest, profit, and a disregard for the environment. The game generated so much controversy in Canada that it was pulled from the TVO website. The major criticism was that the game encouraged players to play as ecoterrorist bombers, which was not the designers' intent in creating the game.[4]

Examples of the serious games genre are often criticized for being didactic. They usually are consigned to the educational rather than entertainment sector and have been accused of not being fun to play. In the past, this criticism has been warranted, particularly when content elements are chosen solely to express values. Increasingly sophisticated games for impact have become more successful as they involve a number of game elements in the quest for meaning making.

Case: *Profit Seed*

In *Profit Seed* (Tiltfactor 2008), designers implemented values through interface, character, rewards, and rules for interaction with the environment. The game mechanics require players to control gusts of wind to move seeds to particular fields on a farm. Some seeds are organic, and some are genetically modified organisms (GMOs). The wind mechanic mimics the real-world ways in which pollen and genetically modified seeds fall on the lands of organic farmers. If a mixture of organic and GMO seeds is found on a plot of land, the farmer will be exposed to litigation—a situation that has happened in the real world. In the game, a lawyer arrives and issues a summons to the player. The game elements of interface (the wind) and character (the farmer, the lawyer, the seeds) allow players to explore the values of private and intellectual property, sustainability, and fairness.

Case: *World of Warcraft*

Consider the value of cooperation. A designer might be able to achieve cooperative behavior within a multiplayer online game by imposing constraints on what actions players can perform or by motivating them with certain rewards. In *World of Warcraft* (Blizzard Entertainment 2004), designers implemented values through player actions, context of play, and rules for interaction with nonplayable characters. In the early days of *World of Warcraft*, raids against end-bosses required mass cooperative efforts of up to forty online players to succeed. This required synchronous participation among many players who sometimes lived in different time zones and had busy lives. Nonetheless, they made this event an important priority to achieve the goal. In a sense, this was a virtual barn raising in which players joined together to complete a task that would be impossible to achieve alone. Groups like the Angry guild, a *World of Warcraft* Horde guild, have a long and well-documented history in successful massive efforts (figure 6.2).[5]

Figure 6.2
Forty members of the Angry guild, assembled to attempt a raid on the Twin Emperors, from *World of Warcraft* (Blizzard Entertainment 2004).

While changing designs in the game require fewer players to complete such raids, experienced players who complete heroic mode raids as a team continue to receive the best rewards. Success is rewarded with some of the game's most desirable gear. Coordinating many players is a challenge, but the value of cooperation is successfully implemented through the elements of rewards, strategies, and rules for interaction with other players.

Case: *Shadow of the Colossus*

Shadow of the Colossus (Sony Computer Entertainment 2005) is another game that implements cooperation and the related value of coordination. In *Shadow of the Colossus*, the designer implemented values through player choices and rules for interaction with other characters. Game designer Fumito Ueda expressed these values by choosing an open-ended form of play rather than giving specific instructions to players. The playable character, Wander, develops a deep relationship with his guide horse, Agro. The horse's behavior, however, is programmed, so she does not always respond to commands. Players therefore cannot "drive" the horse as they would drive a car that reacts precisely to their movements. The player must ride the horse in a two-way relationship that is governed by give and take. This control style leads the player to adopt a cooperative mindset. Companionship and collaboration are values inherent in the Wander/Agro relationship. In Ueda's words, "A real horse … doesn't always obey. It's not like a car or a motorcycle; it won't always turn when you say 'turn!'"[6] The game elements that are relevant here—player choice and rules for interaction with nonplayable characters—allowed Ueda to manifest particular values in *Shadow of the Colossus*.

Other games strike more directly at shaping certain types of behavior. Designer options for implementing such values fall on a continuum. On one end (the coercive end), they may achieve certain behaviors through force (or tight constraints). The game might not allow certain actions to be performed because of the rules for interaction with the environment or for interaction with nonplayable characters or other players. In a maze, players might be able to choose only two paths, three weapons, four actions, five targets, and so forth. On the other end of the continuum (the cooperative end), designers may encourage certain behaviors while still allowing players to exercise choice. This is possible by drawing on known motivators or rewards (such as points, penalties, and levels), feedback (sensory cues with direct pleasant or unpleasant associations), and cues with certain meanings (such as a doorway, a green or red light, the sound of an explosion, and so on). Among approaches to shaping player choices, some are best conceived as obstacles, and others as facilitators. For the latter, designers lead players to engage in certain behaviors by making them easy, inviting, or attractive.

Case: *Farm Blitz*

In *Farm Blitz* (Financial Entertainment 2010), designers tried to implement values through character, player actions, and narrative premise and goals. *Farm Blitz*, from the Doorways to Dreams Fund, is a financial literacy game that combines elements from two popular games, *Bejeweled* (PopCap Games 2001) and *FarmVille* (Zynga 2009a), to promote good savings habits and discourage the accumulation of debt (figure 6.3). The player's goal is to slow down the Bunnies (which multiply as rapidly as debt does) and to grow trees (which increase in size as slowly as money in a savings account does). The game creatively implements values as game elements by using common knowledge—that rabbits multiply rapidly—as its central metaphor. Thus, the character element helps demonstrate the dangers of owing money, and the player's attempts to slow down the Bunnies (the player actions element) matches the real-world behavior that the game hopes to promote (to slow spending). The game breaks with common game goals, which usually focus on rapid accumulation (of money, treasure, or points). The unusual game action of limiting growth (of Bunnies and debt) might prompt a player to question the excessive pursuit of material possessions.

Figure 6.3
A scene from *Farm Blitz* (Financial Entertainment 2010).

Case: *POX: Save the People*

In *POX: Save the People* (Tiltfactor 2010), designers tried to implement values through player actions, rewards, narrative premise and goals, and rules for interaction with the environment. Mary Flanagan's team created the *POX: Save the People* board game, one of Tiltfactor's public health games, to teach systems thinking and generate experiential and analytical responses to vaccination, herd immunity, and the spread of disease (figure 6.4). The team created the original game and two other games. *ZOMBIEPOX* (Tiltfactor 2012) was an identical game with a different narrative premise, and the other was an iPad direct translation of the original game. The goal was to use a strong narrative premise and fantasy to allow players to consider the world around them in different ways, although several public health officials and teachers thought that the narrative's strong fiction would teach far less than a more straightforward design. The results of this implementation are discussed in the next chapter.[7]

Values in Conflict

In the midst of a deadline, a West Coast veteran game designer, "Lorenzo" shared his thoughts on values and game design tradeoffs: "Almost all the games I've worked on have involved noncontroversial subject matter. I've never done a shooter, so you don't have an obvious conflict there in values—i.e., killing people." But he noted that there seems to be a real conflict in values in the commercial models in game design across most types of games. A basic conflict often arises between a designer's creative interest (to make an authentically creative work) and a publisher's economic interest.

Figure 6.4
Two board games—*ZOMBIEPOX* (Tiltfactor 2012) and *POX* (Tiltfactor 2010).

Lorenzo said, "Recent games I've been working on have been 'free to play' games, so the teams had to acquire some pretty awesome chops within game economies. There is definitely a fine line, though, between a cool game and a money sinkhole. We just launched a poker game and have amazing data coming from it. Right after the beta launch, there was one guy who by the second day had spent $700 on the game and had gotten to level 100. This meant he did not put down the game for 48 hours. Is that OK? Or not?" Lorenzo noted that he frequently works with publishers who want simple reskins of existing games with their own content. Game designers often avoid making direct clones because the work is not very creative. Publishers, however, tend to think that such games are cheaper to build and a safer bet with audiences; they pose less risk. So is cloning an existing game model a good idea that responds to what is naturally fun, or is it an uncreative practice that steals the ideas of others?

Any functioning artifact is the product of interacting (and sometimes conflicting) constraints, including physical, economic, and functional constraints. Values may interact with other constraints but also with one another. Values clash in technology design no less than they do in politics, and the variety of these interactions is limitless. Conflicts are not necessarily the results of clumsiness, lack of insight, or dullness but are the inevitable result of a commitment to values' pluralism. We find inspiration in the words of the great political philosopher Isaiah Berlin, who offers a classic assessment of values in conflict:

What is clear is that values can clash—that is why civilizations are incompatible. They can be incompatible between cultures, or groups in the same culture, or between you and me. You believe in always telling the truth, no matter what; I do not, because I believe that it can sometimes be too painful and too destructive. We can discuss each other's point of view, we can try to reach common ground, but in the end what you pursue may not be reconcilable with the ends to which I find that I have dedicated my life. Values may easily clash within the breast of a single individual; and it does not follow that, if they do, some must be true and others false. Justice, rigorous justice, is for some people and absolute value, but it is not compatible with what may be no less ultimate values for them—mercy, compassion—as arises in concrete cases.

Both liberty and equality are among the primary goals pursued by human beings through many centuries; but total liberty for wolves is death to the lambs, total liberty of the powerful, the gifted, is not compatible with the right to a decent existence of the weak and the less gifted.... Equality may demand the restraint of the liberty of those who wish to dominate; liberty—without some modicum of which there is no choice and therefore no possibility of remaining human as we understand the word—may have to be curtailed in order to make room for social welfare, to feed the hungry, to clothe the naked, to shelter the homeless, to leave room for the liberty of others, to allow justice or fairness to be exercised.[8]

Berlin insists that clashing values are not an unusual condition of political and ethical decision making but are inherent to the pluralistic approach to values that he espouses. In each year's docket of U.S. Supreme Court cases, Americans may witness this unending succession of constitutional values in conflict. Even reductionists such as utilitarians, who hold that different values can be reduced to a single value such as happiness or money, cannot avoid conflicts that arise when a decision affects different actors differently. It is not surprising, therefore, to find that design projects (particularly those with multiple requirements, goals, constituencies, and constraints) are rife with clashes and conflicts. These include safety versus cost, transparency versus privacy, aesthetics versus functionality, security versus ease of use, ease of use versus depth, novelty versus familiarity, and entertainment versus education. Clashes may occur across values and across people because choices made in the design and operation of a system affect various people differently.

What is a designer to do? In practical ethics, law, moral philosophy, and politics, resolving values in conflict remains one of the most intractable challenges.[9] Values at Play does not offer an across-the-board solution for problems that for millennia have perplexed lawmakers and philosophers, but this does not mean that designers should throw up their hands in despair, concluding that these hard problems might as well be dealt with arbitrarily or simply ignored. In our view, there is much to be gained by staying alert to design decisions that give rise to such conflicts and to confront them with humility but systematically. Fortunately, not all conflicts are utterly intractable, and although all may not be solved perfectly, they may be eased and mitigated.

For designers who confront hard choices involving a clash of values, the Values at Play heuristic outlines three approaches—dissolving, compromising, and trading off. Dissolving, the happiest of the three, involves finding a creative redesign that provides an alternative pathway for avoiding a particular conflict. When dissolving is impossible, compromise is an alternative that promotes each of the values in question but in less than full measure. Finally, a tradeoff may be necessary, in which one or some values are sacrificed in favor of others.

Dissolving

Dissolving a conflict means developing a creative redesign that achieves all values in question. Too often this option is overlooked because systems developers sometimes fail to see that conflicts are due not to fundamentally incompatible values but to contingent material constraints and uninspired designs. Sometimes this may be achieved by revising prior decisions or choosing different engines or infrastructures because some conflicts may be mere material artifacts or simply poor or rushed design. At times, users and producers of technology resign themselves to making hard choices that may be convenient for incumbents to perpetuate (some conflicts include privacy versus security, anonymity versus accountability, and usability versus functionality). In fact in many concrete instances, what designers face is not so much a brute clash of values, but a narrowing of alternatives due to prior decisions, which in turn reflect uninspired design or, simply, the state of the art of those times.[10] In both cases, revisiting prior decisions might be productive, particularly if the state of the art or science has advanced. Computer designers who previously scratched their heads over the conflict between portability and power, for example, benefit from advances in miniaturization, which greatly eased (if not entirely dissolved) this conflict. Another example is usability, considered an inevitable casualty of complex systems; this conflict can often be dissolved with the help of new visualization techniques, which make it possible to present large and complex data patterns in ways that are comprehensible to users. At times, unimaginative conceptualization is more of a problem than inherent incompatibility of ends. In the realm of games, skeptics may dismiss the idea of values in games and believe that games can either be fun or have deep intentions but not both. Values at Play is an approach to design that aims to dissolve this conflict by demonstrating games that are fun to play and also embody desired values.

The *Peeps* (RAPUNSEL 2006) game project illustrates how conflicts can be dissolved through creative thinking. The designers were developing a three-dimensional dance game that taught basic programming concepts to middle-school girls.[11] The concept was to embed programming code in clothing so that the code, via the clothing used, changed characters' dance moves. Because the game's point of view would shape the relationship between the player and the game world's inhabitants, the designers chose a top-down, God's-eye view. They were concerned, however, that this point of view might lead players to consider their relationship to playable characters in terms of a master-slave dynamic. Rather than abandon the top-down point of view (which might sacrifice playability), they discouraged the master-slave interpretation by changing another element in the game. By inserting a handful of simple artificial intelligence techniques, they provided characters in the game with a degree of autonomy from the player's control. For example, the character offered her own expressions and made comments without the aid of the player. In this way, the playable character was scripted as a semiautonomous agent rather than as a slave to the player's commands. The designers were concerned about the values that might be conveyed through the point-of-view element, so to avoid compromising the quality of the play experience, they implemented some small patterns that were programmed into the behavior of the character. This allowed the designers to offer a God's-eye viewpoint that respected the autonomy of the character. By tinkering with rules for interaction (and not allowing total control of characters in the game), they avoided a problematic interpretation that might otherwise be encouraged by a top-down view of the game world.

Compromising

Where dissolving a conflict is impossible, compromise might be the best alternative. This means promoting each of the values in question but to a possibly unequal extent. Such compromises are so ubiquitous that we hardly even recognize them as such. One familiar illustration is security routines at airports: both liberty and security are compromised as we are scanned and probed. Liberty is certainly compromised, but security is not achieved to its fullest extent because authorities understand that certain effective probes and scans would be unacceptable to passengers. Values compromises are frequently found in popular commercial games. In the original and first expansion pack of *World of Warcraft* (Blizzard Entertainment 2004), players often participated in "capture the flag" minigames that involved ten players from the Horde and another ten from the Alliance. Participation depended on a player's level. Players in levels 10 through 19 were grouped together, as were players in levels 20 through 29, and so on. Some players, however, became the most powerful character at the upper level of the bracket and then chose to remain within that bracket and not advance. They were willing to forego experience points to retain their powers and their advanced weaponry within the lower bracket. Less skilled players were at a significant disadvantage when entering this battleground. They often were killed immediately and sent to the nearby graveyard, temporarily eliminating them from play. New players had little reason to try to fight at their level because game rules favored the more experienced players who stayed in the bracket to take advantage of the weak. The value of fairness was in conflict with the value of player autonomy.

Blizzard resolved the conflict through several decisions. First, designers introduced experience points in the battlegrounds, which gave new players more reason to play. The system also monitored progress so that players who had played before at top levels earned enough experience points to move up to the next bracket. After these changes were made, high-level characters complained because they wanted to assert their seniority with their advanced weapons and powers. Blizzard allowed them to "turn off" such experience points (for an in-game fee) when in the battleground, but the game now sent all players whose experience points were hidden to their own special battleground. This compromise allowed new players to progress and experienced players to wield their power. Finally, Blizzard increased the number of brackets so that each included only five levels of players rather than ten, thus reducing the drastic differences in experience among players. Thus, by changing the elements of rewards and rules for interaction with other players, the game designers preserved the values of equity and opportunity for new players and individuality and autonomy for more experienced players.

Trading Off

In cases where compromise is neither feasible nor desirable, a third option is to trade off—to give up one or some values in favor of others. To return to the example of airport security, advanced imaging technology machines, known as full-body scanners, have been widely criticized, in part for health risks from exposure to the rays but mostly because of the detailed view that they offer of a person's body. These body scanners have traded off modesty and possibly health for security (although skeptics say even security is not achieved). To mitigate, passengers are offered the alternative of avoiding the tradeoff by opting for a body frisk.[12]

We could end the story here but a later turn offers insight into how conflicts can be successfully approached. In 2011, mindful of the uneasy tradeoff, the Transportation Security Administration (TSA) announced that a new software was being installed on its millimeter wave advanced imaging technology (AIT) machines. Instead of producing a detailed body image, the new scanners produced a generic human outline that highlighted possible threats. John Pistole of the TSA was quoted as saying, "This software upgrade enables us to continue providing a high level of security through advanced imaging technology screening, while improving the passenger experience at checkpoints."[13] Assuming that the system works as claimed, the upgrade constitutes progress: the early scanners traded modesty for security, but the upgraded version recovers modesty while maintaining security. In our terms, this innovation successfully dissolves an uncomfortable conflict between these two values.[14]

To return to the world of games, and specifically to the RAPUNSEL project's *Peeps* game,[15] and discuss character representation. The appearance of a character (its size, clothing, sex, build, and ethnicity) contributes significant meaning to a game. Because even something as basic as whether game characters are male or female is a huge marker of difference, the game's design team decided to try out gender-neutral abstract shapes as characters. But after conducting an online survey to collect player feedback, the team realized that their plan had not worked. Many players perceived the shapes as male, and middle-school girls complained that the shapes "just aren't … cool enough." Players who were surveyed overwhelmingly preferred overtly sexualized female figures rather than other types of female characters, abstract shapes, and animals. Players tied their preferences to the products and services that they already used. The players' favorite character was a cartoon girl from a popular fashion website because, as one eleven-year-old put it, she was a "cool girl … she's modern, art-time; she has attitude."[16] In such a situation, most design teams would happily give in, quoting the old gaming mantra "Give the players what they want." What players want, however, has been shaped by their consumption of television shows, films, and other games and often embeds unwelcome values. Is it acceptable to perpetuate a stereotype in order to please players? Instead, the design team resisted stereotypes, went back into development, and through tradeoff and compromise created a sportier and less sexualized character.

PeaceMaker (ImpactGames 2007), the Israeli-Palestinian conflict game discussed in chapter 3, features a different sort of tradeoff. The narrative premise of the game, achieving peace, is rarely without conflict. To start, players take on a character role (either the Palestinian president or the Israeli prime minister) in the middle of the conflict. The game goal is for either side to produce a two-state solution to the conflict. By incorporating real-life videos and images rather than cartoons, the game adds dramatic tension and a better sense of the stakes. Players choose actions, from aggressive to cooperative, but they soon learn that the conflict is exacerbated by aggression and violence. The game triggers empathy on both cognitive and emotional levels.[17] Because the player initially has to take sides, the values of community and loyalty are woven into the role of the playable character—and yet those values can be at odds with the goal of the game. The player can play the game from the opposite character and see how the same values affect what was once the enemy. The solution in this game lies in giving up aggression and compromising one's own most valued principles—home, community, loyalty—so that others can enjoy their own experience of those same values. The actual conflict of values is embedded into the game fabric, and a solution often seems impossible, which makes for a unique case.

Implementation for Designers

Implementation involves translating values into game architecture and features. Values at Play does not supersede the creative act of design. Instead, it offers guideposts to designers. One approach is to look to key game elements as potential sites for shaping values. Another is to consider potential modes of connecting with players to encourage certain behaviors, challenge beliefs and attitudes, or induce certain affective responses. By considering game elements, designers may find inspiration for implementation challenges. Ambitious designers undoubtedly will confront values conflicts. These are inevitable in most complex systems, and games are no exception; such is the nature of games, of technological artifacts, and of the moral universe.

Not all conflicts, however, are intractable. Values at Play provides three questions that designers can ask to help them navigate the quagmire of values conflicts: Can the conflict be dissolved? Is compromise possible? Must some values be traded off in favor of others? Translating big-picture values into nitty-gritty decisions is never easy. But through careful attention to the full spectrum of game elements, modes of intervention with players, and awareness of the possibility of conflicts, designers can take the values they discovered and implement them within the game world.

Values in Game Hardware

by Kyle Rentschler

In our day-to-day lives, we encounter many designed objects, from the utensils that we use to eat to the cars that we drive. Although we often overlook the design of these objects or how their design affects us, even simple observations of the most mundane objects reveal those objects to be deliberately constructed around human values. For instance, the design for small, dull, brightly colored children's scissors is different than the design for large, sharp, industrial-looking adult's scissors, probably for self-apparent reasons such as safety, accessibility, and visual appeal. Such analyses also pertain to objects that are associated with play. Lincoln Logs, for example, recall nature, austerity, and American history in their look and feel, and Legos seem to be designed around modernism and modularity. In turn, each type of building block also affords uses that parallel their physical details. Lincoln Logs seem restricted to what actual logs are capable of building, and Legos allow for a wider variety of structures. Although Lincoln Logs and Legos might initially seem like homologous toys, they provide different play experiences. Values are similarly embedded in video game hardware, which is the material component of today's most prominent mass-mediated playgrounds.

But before turning to a discussion of how values are embedded in video game hardware design, we have to address an important question: what is hardware? *Hardware* is a tricky term with a sinuous past. It was first used in the fifteenth century to denote small metal goods, and for hundreds of years its original definition remained unchanged. The use of the term hardware in terms of household appliances fits into this original definition. However, an additional definition of *hardware* emerged in the late 1940s—"the physical components of a computer system." Video games appropriated this term from early computing and its hardware/software bifurcation. In other words, hardware is those physical parts of the video game that players interact with in the material world. Video game hardware generally includes the platforms that are used to run game software (such as a desktop PC, a Nintendo DS, or a Sony PlayStation 3), and controllers and the peripheral equipment that players use to play the game (such as a keyboard, a video game controller, or an iPhone touch screen).

Video game hardware is a designed object, and the various types of hardware are prototyped and actualized by teams of professional designers. Popular video game companies spend millions of dollars on the research, production, and marketing of their hardware, and they put a lot of thought into its design. Up and down the production line, video game designers make decisions about both hardware and software. Sometimes these decisions seem exclusive to either software or hardware, such as deciding the genre that a game will fall into or selecting the materials that will be used to build a console. However, most decisions are not exclusive to either the hardware or software components of a game. Indeed, decisions made on the design room floor about hardware often take software into consideration and vice versa.

Although many hardware designers are aware of how hardware technologically influences software, popular rhetoric surrounding game design often relegates hardware design to the back burner. It may be helpful to think of hardware and software as coconstituting the game and hardware and software design as coconstituting game design. If we want to talk about game design, we have to recognize the integral role that hardware plays. For economic purposes, it makes sense for the game industry to reuse hardware platforms, so that not every game requires a new console or controller. Perhaps in part because of this, hardware is often taken for granted in considering the overarching play experience of a particular game. On the other hand, many indie games and a handful of commercial games often use unique hardware that was designed specifically with the software in mind. Mary Flanagan has shown the important role that is played by hardware in *[giantJoystick]* (2006), where players must collaborate to control a ten-foot tall joystick to play classic Atari games. This unconventional control scheme not only draws attention to hardware as an integral part of game design but also fundamentally alters the experience of playing the game.

Similarly, the play experience in *Dance Dance Revolution* (Konami 1998) is as contingent on the hardware as it is on the software. By the late 1990s, consumers were avoiding public arcades in favor of private home consoles. Arcade developers scrambled for the next hit, and Konami drew from a rich history of innovative arcade hardware to bring the burgeoning rhythm genre to arcades with a fresh control scheme. *Dance Dance Revolution* was the first of many dance games that replace the traditional controller with four directional arrows on the ground. Konami decided that this hardware would be well suited for arcade play, attracting onlookers to the machine as both audience members and potential players. The game turned out to be a huge hit. Although *Dance Dance Revolution*'s mechanics are similar to preceding rhythm games—such as *PaRappa the Rappa* (NanaOn-Sha 1996), which requires players to tap the buttons of the PlayStation controller in sync with the rhythm of music—it differs in how the player pushes the buttons. Instead of playing the game inertly from a seat, players are required to move their entire bodies, and because the game is played in an arcade setting, this often takes place in front of groups of other people. The game quickly gained a reputation for encouraging physical fitness and possibly helping players become better dancers, and a devout cult following of dynamic individuals added elements of performativity. The biggest shift from early rhythm games to *Dance Dance Revolution* is the hardware itself—the arcade cabinet design and its constituent control scheme. Although *Dance Dance Revolution* and its predecessors intimately share many gameplay mechanics, the change in hardware drastically changes the phenomenological experience of playing. What could have been a trite and briefly popular game genre endures to this day, and its popularity ebbs and flows in cycles that often are based on hardware innovation, such as the *SingStar* (London Studios 2004) microphone or *Guitar Hero* (Red Octane/Activision 2005) guitar. The popularity of an entire commercial genre of games is predicated on hardware.

As shown by the above example, hardware can be designed with software while the overarching game is being designed. Throughout the development of hardware, designers can imbue it with values. Because most game hardware is developed with commercial interests in mind, values such as accessibility, ease of use, approachability, expense, and ergonomics are often taken into consideration in popular hardware such as the iPhone or Nintendo Wii. Even industry standards, such as the proliferation of first-person shooters over the past decade, have influenced the design of modern controllers. Indeed, popular types of games influence the development of hardware. The Xbox 360 S controller, for example, was designed with first-person shooters in mind. Sometimes, hardware is not developed most profitably the first time around. The original Xbox controller, for example, was often seen as being too large and cumbersome for small hands. In response, Microsoft imported its smaller Japanese market controller as the default controller in the United States, giving a wider range of players access to games on that platform. Accessibility and equality were not taken into account in the initial design but were foregrounded in a later version.

Potentially every designed object has values embedded in it, but sometimes it is easier to locate values in atypical artifacts because they are not the norm. One example of an unusual piece of hardware is the cabinet of Atari's early maze game, *Gotcha!* (Atari 1973). *Gotcha!* was Atari's fourth game and one of the first examples of the maze game genre, but it is perhaps best remembered for its arcade cabinet joysticks. Due to what is rumored to have been an inside joke at Atari about joysticks resembling phalluses, early versions of *Gotcha!* implemented rubber domes that simulated breasts. To play the game, the player squeezes these mounds to navigate the maze. The public responded negatively to the release of the game, and subsequent versions of the game used regular joysticks. However, as one of the many 1970s arcade cabinets to experiment with hardware interface design, it is remembered for its overhanded integration of sexuality and the female body. In the designers' intentions, the actual design of the cabinet, and in the public's subsequent outcry, we can see how designing hardware with certain values in mind can be interpreted as controversial, abnormal, explicit, lewd, and sexual.

On the other hand, sometimes hardware has been praised for the values that it seems to promote. With the rise of casual gaming, some hardware has been lauded for its accessibility and ease of use. Although the Nintendo Wii and Nintendo DS are good examples of this, the surge of the iPhone as a gaming platform perhaps best typifies what it means to design hardware around values like accessibility. Although many nongamers have long considered console controllers an intimidating barrier to entry, the iPhone has helped spawn a new market of gamers who play on the go in short bursts. The iPhone is unintimidating, builds off knowledge that the player has acquired by using the phone in its other capacities, and appears to be easier to use than other gaming devices because of its touch screen. Because Apple has historically designed its products around values such as ease of use, we can see how these values have been translated to video game hardware design. Indeed, the value-embedded design of video game hardware has become relevant not only to aficionados or to hardcore gamers who might search for an old *Gotcha!* cabinet, but to everyday users of our most pervasive technology.

These two examples demonstrate how values have been embedded in the design of past hardware. Looking forward, we can predict that there will be an increased awareness of hardware design in the game industry. As video game design becomes more and more scrutinized, the possibility of intentionally designing hardware around select human values emerges as a distinct possibility. Whatever this hardware turns out to be, we will be able to learn from it, as we have from past hardware. Just as play doesn't take place only on the screen, the values at play do not exist only within the monitors where we play digital games. They also exist in what we use to play them—in those pieces of the game that exist in the material world. We need to understand hardware as part of the game itself, and when we talk about values in games, we need to understand the role that is played by hardware in establishing these values. This allows us to have a more nuanced understanding of games, expect more of ourselves as consumers, demand more of ourselves as designers, and inspire deeper thought and reflection on whatever we create. By taking this values-conscious step, we make ourselves more mindful players and designers.

7   Verification

After discovering and implementing values, conscientious designers will want to answer a key question: did it work? Verification involves assessing whether efforts to integrate values have succeeded. As is suggested in chapter 4, an iterative process means that this question—verification—should not be reserved for the very end of production but asked at every step of the way.

Verification is crucial to any technological system. It is relatively simple to verify that a toaster achieves its aim of browning bread evenly without blowing a fuse. It is somewhat more difficult to verify that a Web search engine finds what users are seeking. Verifying values in games poses even greater challenges, primarily because assessment must take into account the complex interdependencies among the game (as artifact), its players, and the context of play. Verifying also must confront a different type of challenge from skeptics who ask, "Do you really think that playing a game can save the environment, bring about world peace, or make individuals kinder, more sensitive, and less biased?" Responding to these challenges means describing how Values at Play might be verified (the primary task of this chapter) and identifying what is being verified (what designers mean when they say that a game embodies, expresses, promotes, or supports a given value or set of values). One method for discovering whether a game that promotes energy conservation actually embodies conservation might be to measure players' energy conservation before and after playing the game; luckily for the complex range of methods there are also other methods.

The substantive contribution of this chapter extends beyond our review of processes for verifying claims made about values at play. We also aim to broaden the understanding of what it means, in the first place, to claim that values are 'in' a given game. We suggest three interpretations for this claim: One, noted above, is as a claim about the ways in which players' behaviors, practices, activities, and ways of doing are affected. A second is whether the game expands and deepens players' understanding and appreciation of target values and closely allied issues. And, a third is the extent of a game's systematic impact on players' attitudes, empathy, or affect.

This chapter discusses various ways that designers might proceed with the verification process. Drawing on standard practices followed in game design, in software systems development more generally, and in social sciences research, it reviews methods that designers might adopt, concluding with real-world situations in which designers put research methods to work in conducting verification.

The Verification Process

According to the iterative design process introduced in chapter 4 (see figure 4.1, A traditional game development cycle), the usual steps in designing a video game are planning, review of requirements, analysis and design, implementation, and finally, verification. The process is cyclical, involving constant review and testing to ensure that the final products meet the initial demands. Even in the earliest stages of a project, verification occurs as initial versions are play-tested by various groups. Most familiar to game designers is testing via prototypes,[1] which are highly useful in experimenting with particular parts of a given game and the values that emerge.[2] In technical scenarios, modes from agile programming might aid in systems for which requirements change frequently.[3]

Within an iterative process, there are a number of ways to conduct verification. In engineering and software development, the process is often referred to as validation and verification (V&V). Various criteria can be used to ensure that a given artifact fulfills its objectives. The first major criterion is functional: Did we build the right thing? Did we build the house or digital game that the customer wanted? Is the kitchen in the spot where the customer wanted it to be? Does the game play the way that it was supposed to? This might seem to be the core question, but there is more to the process. Continuing with the kitchen example, sometimes when you put the kitchen in the spot where the customer wants it, there is unfortunately no place to put the exhaust fan that is required by building codes. Thus, the second criterion in reviewing a work is experiential: Did we build it right? Is the house's construction of high quality, and does it conform to building codes? Does the game's software operate in all required browsers?

Figure 7.1 shows the types of verification that are considered in the standard software design cycle: requirements of the system are reviewed and verified, the design is verified, the actual code and hardware are created and verified, and the process itself undergoes review. Many nuances are involved in traditional software verification, but the values that appear in traditional verification involve only the "useful" values of reliability, efficiency, and robustness. When human values are involved, validation must go beyond these categories of assessment. Each category must be augmented to bring values into account.

New questions about values in games need to be added to the traditional strands of verification. As noted in chapter 4, the Values at Play model inserts values into the iterative software design process, so the conscientious designer must plan the project with values in mind, discover what values are at play, implement those values in the design of the game, and verify that the values discovered and implemented are expressed in the game. When ideas surface from this iterative model, designers must map player patterns and feedback to each of the game's elements. Although values emerge from the many game elements, these are best verified together in their cumulative effect.

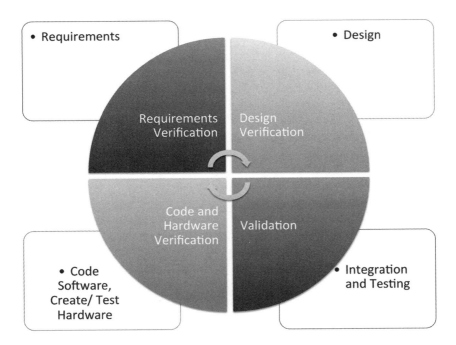

Figure 7.1
Software verification through an engineering lens.

Verification that values are embodied in the software or game might be facilitated through regular meetings with design partners, play-testers, educators, outside peers, and industry advisers. Designers must ensure that the game improves with the tight integration of values and that the values do not drop out of the game. This is a delicate balancing act among seemingly opposing goals; the task that would be impossible without an iterative testing and feedback structure.

Later in the game development process (sometimes after a project is finished), it is wise to conduct formal assessments. The software engineer's question about functionality ("Did we build the right thing?") translates into "Did we incorporate the values discovered at the onset of the project consistently throughout the game in a meaningful way?" That is the easy part. The software engineer's question about experience ("Did we build it right?") is more difficult to address because it involves turning the game loose into the world, having people play it in vastly differing contexts, and seeing how those values are experienced. Trying to understand whether a game changes a behavior (by persuading someone to quit smoking, for example), shapes an attitude (about America's foreign interventions, for instance), or provokes an emotion (such as empathy for genocide victims) requires sophisticated tools of analysis.

Because iterative software design does not have the vocabulary to address questions of values, the conscientious designer must draw from other disciplines. Any given game can contain perspectives from psychology, literature, media studies, education, human factors, and health. In some of these disciplines, verification may take the form of standardized research protocols, which typically follow the scientific method: a researcher identifies a problem, posits a hypothesis or set of research questions, gathers relevant data, and analyzes and interprets the data.

The way in which a researcher gathers data is important. Different disciplines have different research methods, such as ethnographies, experiments, historiographies, and case studies. In the social sciences, research tends to fall into three general categories—quantitative methods, qualitative methods, and hybrid or blended methods. Quantitative methods try to capture the amount of something. They count, collect measurements, and almost always include statistical analyses. Qualitative methods attempt to encompass the qualities of a phenomenon (the how, what, where, when, and why). Qualitative research gathers meaning, context, descriptions, and settings. Both methods stress objectivity and rigor and can offer valid perspectives.

Research on values typically (but not always) involves qualitative research methods. Whether data gathered is quantitative (numerically driven, such as the number of clicks on a given item on screen) or qualitative (nuanced and difficult to compare, such as interviews about player beliefs), what truly matters is that the research is conducted carefully and analyzed rigorously. This model can be applied to values questions, and it can be used with either quantitative or qualitative approaches. A simplified model of a research program is shown in figure 7.2.

Verification research with players is conducted through the two lenses of quantitative research, which relies on vetted methods and numerical markers of individual preference, and qualitative research, which is more descriptive and exploratory. Another way to think about methods is to think of experimental methods versus descriptive methods. Descriptive methods try to get to the root of the issues by providing participants with an intervention and then observing the result.

Experimental methods establish a set of identifiable conditions to which participants are randomly assigned to test the causal relationship between an intervention and an outcome (figure 7.3). For example, when using an experimental study design approach for a particular iPad game, researchers might study a collecting mechanic across different versions of the game that feature a competitive game goal. A control condition (or neutral/no intervention state) provides a baseline for comparison. Ideally, the verification process can combine both approaches: descriptive studies can tell you what appears to be happening with a particular design, and experiments allow designers to test the apparent effects systematically.

Research on values in games typically investigates how players are affected by the experience of playing a game, so both angles—descriptive and experimental—could prove useful. Before beginning the game, players might be given a pretest that includes survey questions or interviews. After playing the game (the intervention), they are given a posttest. Then the pre- and posttests are compared to determine if the game brought about

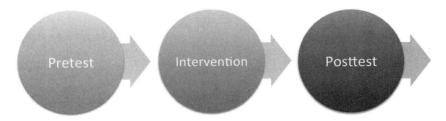

Figure 7.2
A typical pretest and posttest model.

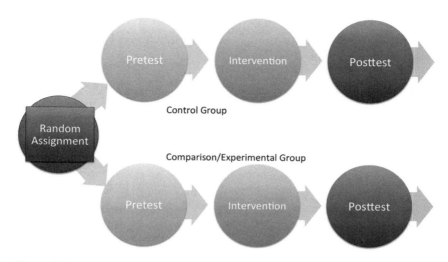

Figure 7.3
An experimental model.

any changes in the players.[4] Ideally, a follow-up study several weeks later would determine if any effects last.

Using qualitative research methods, designers who seek to verify their design execution might conduct deep descriptive work in the form of interviews, observations, video and audio analysis, and longer-term ethnography. During play, think-aloud protocols can be an effective research technique. Players give a running commentary that describes their in-game decisions and their impressions of the game, which helps researchers understand what players think during the play experience. These could be outcomes in themselves, or they could be mediators between the game and the eventual behavior or attitude change. Assessments after play can gather effects of the entire play experience, many of which are not obvious or predictable. Finally, researchers can collect general data by observing a player and detecting technical data (such as time on task or screens, number of clicks, and where clicks occur). Careful researchers seek larger numbers: data collected from two hundred players would be a far stronger data set than data collected from eighteen.

Another approach would be to use an experimental design. In an experimental study design, players are randomly assigned to one of several treatments to determine causal relationships between particular elements of a game's design and changes in player attitudes or behaviors. Some randomly assigned players play one version of the game, and others play slightly different versions in an attempt to isolate the effects of nuanced design decisions in the game. This type of verification allows designers to compare different conditions or differing designs. One group of players plays a control version that is a neutral or value-free variant of the games. Then a variant that includes the values is included as the experimental version. In an experimental design, the players experience only one version of the game; they do not see the other versions of the game during verification.

Using an experimental approach helps the design team remain objective and honestly examine what is happening with players. How the players are addressed is important. They cannot be asked leading questions or be swayed toward particular answers.[5] In any verification process, how players are questioned is pivotal. Asking the right questions in verification is the key to understanding whether values are supported or have changed through a game.

Cases

As noted above, verifying the values at play in a given game covers a variety of relevant outcomes, including whether and to what extent the game affects players' behaviors in ways that are systematically relevant to values of interest, enhances players' understanding and appreciation of the values and associated issues, and changes players' attitudes and evokes relevant affective responses. Verifying these outcomes can take many forms. Questionnaires and testing can reveal some sorts of values contents, but they do not provide deep insight into affective states, such as empathy. To gauge behavioral change such as health interventions, large, randomized controlled trials may be necessary to ensure that the results are taken seriously by the medical and psychological communities. Those who study values in games must adapt their methods to suit both the values in question and the nature of the outcomes hypothesized as dependent variables. In this section, we explore case studies of assessment and verification.

Verification 1: Has the Game Promoted the Desired Behaviors?

Can games change behavior? If we claim that the answer is yes, what evidence do we have to prove it? Behavior change can refer to behaviors in the game as well as outside of it. Within a game, designers might find that particular design choices encourage players in multiplayer environments to collaborate rather than compete or to take risks rather than play it safe. Such in-game behavioral changes are easier to verify than changes beyond the game environment. With games, as with other media, understanding how they affect change in people's behavior is an urgent, ongoing research challenge. As discussed below, health games have been found to change some patient behavior.

Health Games: Values of Exercise, Health, Self-Care, and Autonomy   In a 2007 review article, Tom Baranowski and his colleagues surveyed twenty-eight studies of games that promoted health-related behavior through a variety of techniques such as reminders, tailored messages, goal setting, learning from a game's "life lesson," and so on. Most of the articles found correlations between playing the games and positive behavioral changes.[6] Exercise games showed the most straightforward results. A 2006 study looked at the game *Dance Dance Revolution* (Konami 1998) as played by overweight and nonoverweight children and adolescents and found that it boosted heart rates above the minimum level for cardio fitness.[7] Other studies have had similar results, showing that playing some games involving movement can be counted as exercise for youth.[8] In 1997, Brown, Lieberman, et al. studied the effects of a game for adolescent diabetes. The game, *Packy & Marlon* (WaveQuest/Raya Systems 1995), was an adventure-style Super Nintendo Entertainment System game that was designed to engage diabetic youth in self-care (figure 7.4). Players take the character's blood sugar management and handle food selections for four virtual days. The players played on average a total of thirty-four hours over six months, and the treatment group (game players) experienced a 75 percent drop in emergency and urgent care visits.

Unlike most studies of exercise games that focus on in-game factors such as heart rate, a handful of studies have attempted to demonstrate change in player behavior outside of game environments. An example of this is the effort to verify the effectiveness of Hopelab's *Re-Mission*. Developed in 2006 to 2008, *Re-Mission* was designed to help adolescents and young adults with cancer (including acute leukemia, lymphoma, and soft-tissue sarcoma) to understand and participate in their own care. Study results, which were published in the medical journal *Pediatrics*, showed that playing *Re-Mission* significantly improved key behavioral and psychological factors associated with successful cancer treatment.[9] The study was conducted using a randomized trial among 375 participants who were thirteen to nineteen years old and undergoing treatment at thirty-four different medical centers in the United States, Canada, and Australia. The researchers examined the categories of adherence, self-efficacy, knowledge, control, stress, and quality of life. Patients on particular drugs were tracked by either pill-monitoring devices or blood and urine tests. In the study, participants who played the

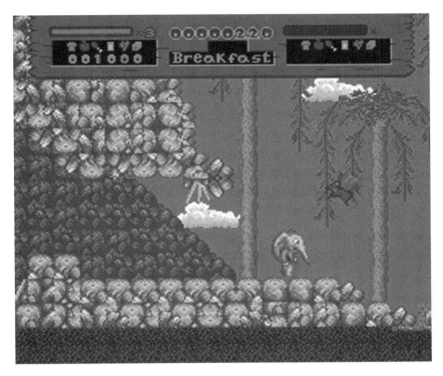

Figure 7.4
A scene from *Packy & Marlon* (WaveQuest/Raya Systems 1995).

game maintained higher levels of chemotherapy in their blood and took their antibiotics more consistently than those in the control group. Participants given *Re-Mission* also showed faster acquisition of cancer-related knowledge. These results indicate that a carefully designed video game can positively affect health behavior in young people with chronic illness. Hopelab's game-integrated portable monitoring device, Zamzee, also shows clinical promise.

Greitemeyer and Osswald (2010) studied the effects of prosocial (socially positive) games on behavior. They used experimental studies and conducted four experiments that examined the hypothesis that playing a prosocial (relative to a neutral) video game increases helping behavior. The team found that exposure to prosocial video games activated prosocial thoughts, which in turn promoted prosocial behavior. These results cast light on the content of video games and demonstrate that content can foster both antisocial and prosocial effects.

Stanford Study: Values of Sustainability and Environmentalism   In a 2011 unpublished study conducted at Stanford, researcher Sun Joo Ahn engaged fifty people as participants in a study about how using nonrecycled paper leads to deforestation.[10] The study's aim was to see if it was possible to change behavior in the physical world. After an initial introduction, half of the participants read a text, which further described what happened to the tree as well as to animals such as birds that depend on the tree. The other twenty-five participants entered a virtual forest and were told to cut down sequoia redwood trees using a game controller that gave haptic feedback so that players could feel the sawing. Before the intervention, regardless of their assigned group, all participants reported a belief that their personal actions could improve the environment and affect sustainability. After the intervention, the researcher staged an accident, spilling water across a table where she had placed a stack of paper napkins. This provided participants with a chance to put their stated beliefs into practice. The subjects grabbed napkins to clean up the spill, and those who had read only about logging used an average of 20 percent more napkins than those who had sawed down trees in the virtual forest. Were the behaviors that the researchers were interested in promoting actually encouraged by playing this game? According to this study, they were. Although this was a small experiment, nearly 90 percent of psychological studies measure immediate impact, as did this small study.

Extrinsic and Intrinsic Rewards in Activist Games   Game makers must be careful about how they structure rewards in a game because the psychology of rewards is complex. In 1973, Lepper, Greene, and Nisbett demonstrated that the experience of play is fragile and can easily turn into its opposite. One way that play can turn into its inverse ("not play" or even work) is to offer rewards. In this study, the researchers observed children engaged in the inherently pleasurable task of drawing. When kids were rewarded for their drawings with prizes such as ribbons or gold stars, they subsequently spent less time playing with drawing materials.[11] Before the reward system, the children were drawing out of a sheer joy: The activity was its own reward. Rewards, however, caused a psychological shift. The children's reasons for drawing became associated with acquiring ribbons and gold stars, and their pleasure in the task declined. The children's intrinsic motivation was replaced by extrinsic motivation, a phenomenon psychologists call the *overjustification effect*. This led to a decrease in the kids' interest in drawing because extrinsic rewards are not nearly as motivating as intrinsic rewards. The research has held up. A 1999 metaanalysis of 128 studies on motivation and rewards found that tangible incentives do reduce intrinsic pleasure in tasks that the participants found inherently compelling.[12] It appears that people feel that their autonomy is compromised by external rewards and that external rewards interfere with the enjoyment of internal rewards from the same activity.

Recent enthusiasm for gamification—the framing of everyday activities within gamelike reward structures—attempts to adopt an approach that is used in programs such as airline miles and the Girl Scout badge system. Gamification has prompted many new companies to hope that behavior change can be transformed into profit. The process will not be simple. Although games are engines for possible behavior change and motivating ultimate intrinsic pleasure, there are also ways to design a game to undermine intrinsic pleasure by externalizing rewards. For designers, the application of a game to a social issue demands a clear alignment between the value and the game design.

One educational game whose success has been proven through rigorous assessment is *Quest Atlantis* (Sasha Barab 2005), a game that consciously integrated values into its design. More than ten thousand children have played the game, and there have been multiple studies of its effects. Student players have demonstrated learning gains in science, language arts, and social studies. More important, teachers and students reported increased levels of engagement and interest in pursuing the curricular issues outside of school. The game helped children find a creative voice to explore global issues, personal feelings, and personal agency. The game managed to activate both internal and external reward systems.[13]

Other games have been less successful. An activist urban mobile game encouraged players to engage with people on the streets of New York City with the goal of promoting a more political sensibility in players and passersby. The game covered subjects such as union strikes, fires, and riots, and one game task was to discover things about certain sites and document the discoveries through photos, videos, and text messages. One player (called Trixie here) found herself in Tompkins Square Park in the East Village. She encountered a man on a park bench, and they discussed the riot that erupted in the park in 1988 when the police tried to remove homeless people who had been sleeping there. The man said that he still lived in the same apartment overlooking the park that he did in 1988. As the two discussed the riots and the way that neighborhood residents responded to them, Trixie became so interested that she nearly forgot the game was in progress. Given that the game was devoted to reinvigorating conversations about the history and politics of the city, this would not necessarily have been an unfortunate outcome. The extrinsic reward of the points dropped off, the external reward replaced by the intrinsic pleasure of connecting to another person and his story.[14]

During this conversation, members of another team appeared and voided Trixie's points by catching her in the act of gathering points. The man on the park bench had been planted by the other team as a lure that would allow them to catch other teams in the process of interacting with residents. In a typical game, such a well-timed 'gotcha' moment would have been a brilliant move. But in a game that fosters the values of communication, community, respect, and solidarity, it was ill-considered because the game rules encouraged players to undermine the game's purported values. As a player, Trixie's intrinsic motivation was lost through the extrinsic reward framework that did not match the values espoused by the game.[15]

To the designers of the game, the event went on mechanically without a hitch. There was a winning team, and people had fun exploring the city. But as a game that was trying to express and support specific values, it failed. Indiscriminate applications of commonly accepted reward systems, mechanics, narrative premises, and other elements in games may not work to support a particular value. A false mapping phenomenon can occur in which the external rewards may undermine the intrinsic values, pleasure, and motivation for a player. If the designers had included the core values of the project in their iterative process and had verified with play-testers that the rules supported the values in the game, the game could have succeeded in its mission.

Verification 2: Have We Have Enabled Greater Understanding and Appreciation?

Shifts in behavior are among the more obvious effects that a game can have. Less obvious, but still measurable, is a change in a player's understanding and appreciation of certain circumstances and relevant values. In the following cases, games were explicitly designed to promote such understanding.

POX: Save the People—Values of Collaboration, Community, and Health   In 2010, the Mascoma Valley Health Initiative, a New Hampshire public health organization, asked the Tiltfactor game design laboratory to create a game to teach the public about the value of vaccination. The group planned to use the game in classrooms and at health fairs to demonstrate the role that vaccines play in preventing the spread of disease. The goal was to promote a better understanding of herd immunity—an immunity that

occurs when a large part of a population is vaccinated against a contagious disease, which helps protect those who might not be able to be vaccinated such as those with immune system disorders. The stakes are high. Because of misunderstandings surrounding vaccinations, many communities in developed countries are losing herd immunity to pernicious illnesses (like whooping cough) that until recently had been nearly banished. The team chose a "collaborative strategy" approach to the design of the game, wherein player cooperation mechanisms would reflect the ways in which members of a community stricken by a health crisis would work together. The team designed the game around the values of collaboration, cooperation, community, and health.

The game, called *POX: Save the People*, was completed in 2011 after a six-month concept-to-completion cycle. The first version was a board game, which later was ported to iPad. The board game is played on a rectangular board of eighty-one spaces (nine rows and nine columns), and each space represents one person in a community where a contagious disease could spread (figure 7.5). At the beginning of the game, two people are immediately infected with a disease. The disease spreads throughout the community with each turn through the direction of randomized game cards, which indicate the direction of the spread for the board. Outbreaks also occur in new areas of the board, just as they might in real life appear in new areas of a city. As the game progresses, players decide to cure those infected or vaccinate to prevent new infections and ultimately halt the disease's progress. Too many deaths in the community cause a player to lose.

In the pilot study of the game, the design team conducted pre- and post-tests for two sessions of gameplay and asked players to write answers to the following question about a different type of health issue:[16]

You are the director of a large public health organization. The rate of HIV infection among adults in your country is greater than 20%. Because their immune systems are weakened, people with HIV cannot be vaccinated against other deadly diseases, such as tuberculosis. Your job is to reduce the vulnerability of this country's HIV+ population to tuberculosis. How would you address this public health problem?

This question was intended to test whether players could transfer their understanding of health issues in *POX: Save the People* to another issue, and the results were surprisingly positive. Most players provided preplay answers that indicated no understanding of herd immunity, but the post-play answers of half of the participants showed that they clearly understood the concept. We also found that players learned about disease prevention and the speed with which disease spreads. Finally, players learned that most

Figure 7.5
A screen showing the results of contagious disease, from *POX: Save the People* (Tiltfactor 2011).

public health departments have only limited resources, even though this message was contained only in the mechanic and not in the game instructions. Although we did not set out to measure for belief change because the game is a relatively short intervention, there were instances of change, as documented in this conversation between two players in the pilot study:

Andy: I don't know if you'd consider that one *Law and Order* episode, but somebody was suing somebody else for not vaccinating their child.
Rayanne: Yeah, I watched that…. The child hadn't been vaccinated, but …
Andy: We watched that together.
Rayanne: … but that was fine, but then the child got another child sick and that child died.
Andy: Yeah. I was like, "Not OK." … We had a nice discussion about that …
Rayanne: Whether you should be forced to vaccinate your kids. I think I believe I took a side of "Yes."
Andy: I took a side of "No," but it makes sense to be "Yes."

Although information alone does not change behavior, interacting with the information may indeed change attitudes, beliefs, and behavior. These productive interactions may heighten the importance of playing with values. The *POX* game helped players to understand herd immunity and supported health, community, and cooperation as core values. In addition to the formal verification described above, designers of course are also play-testing their game for gameplay; a designer knows that their games are working if they are testing well. We tested the game hundreds of times at venues such as the Gen Con, a table top gaming convention that attracts nearly fifty thousand gamers annually (figure 7.6).

In a follow up study, our team compared playing the original game to two other conditions—*ZOMBIEPOX* (Tiltfactor 2012), which was an identical board game with a different narrative layer, and the iPad direct translation of *POX: Save the People*. Through randomized controlled studies, we measured systems thinking, understanding of disease spread and immunity, and valuation of vaccine. Across all research questions, the most effective game was *ZOMBIEPOX*, and the game with the least effective results was the iPad version of *POX: Save the People*. (All conditions were statistically significantly better than the control state or no game at all.)

Few studies tease out the efficacy of the affordances of digital games as compared to other game forms. In this set of studies, the iPad *POX* game was less effective than the board game *ZOMBIEPOX* for the transference of core learning principles.

Verification 3: Have We Have Elicited a Particular Affective or Attitudinal Response?

Through games, designers have the power to alter a player's perspective of the world and disrupt habitual attitudes and affective responses. The games that are discussed in this section were designed to promote empathy by altering players' perspective on their subjects' plight.

Layoff: **The Value of Empathy**   Tiltfactor created *Layoff* (2009) to look at values related to the U.S. financial crisis of the time.[17] In this tile-matching puzzle video game, players take on the role of corporate managers who are cutting jobs (figure 7.7). It was intended to stir empathy for laid-off workers, to alter players' comprehension of an important social phenomenon, and perhaps even to incite indignation against the unjust distribution of suffering across social and economic classes.

In the original version of *Layoff*, which featured images of workers as anonymous, nameless characters, players seemed to enjoy laying people

Figure 7.6
Players interacting with the board game *POX: Save the People* (Tiltfactor 2010).

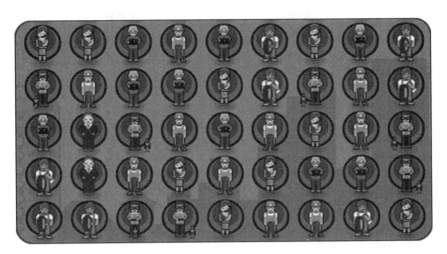

Figure 7.7
Workers from *Layoff* (Tiltfactor 2009).

off. They exhibited little empathy for the workers or introspection about the financial crisis. Because these results did not achieve the goals set by the team, the designers decided to further humanize the workers, writing short character biographies. By tweaking the elements of character and player choice, the designers successfully implemented their values goals. Players discussed which characters could survive a layoff more easily than others and reflected on their own jobs and personal histories. Players contemplated workplace hiring and firing practices, experienced them as arbitrary and cruel, and considered how these practices deeply affected the fates of individuals.

After the game's release, national news media treated *Layoff* as controversial, and an NBC News reporter interviewed people on the street, asking questions like "What do you think of a game where you play by laying workers off?" This leading question, asked of people who were unfamiliar with the game, elicited the expected negative comments, and many people replied that a game should "not be making fun" of layoffs. The news piece went on to adopt a more nuanced approach and compared the game to the work of Charlie Chaplin, noting that during "hard times" much valuable discussion and solidarity can arise from media experiences.

Players of the game confirmed that it had real emotional impact, and the team utilized the game as a research tool to study empathy in games. How do players feel about layoffs in the game and in their community? Do they cognitively link the two? In our research, we found that players empathetically linked to the workers in the game on both cognitive and emotional levels. A twenty-eight-year-old male gamer from Michigan said that reading the personal information about workers made him "kind of sad":

> They become real people and it becomes hard to lay them off. Maybe I just feel this way because it hits close to home. This week is my last week at my relatively decent and moderately good paying job before I get put on an "indefinite" layoff. Unemployment rate is 11.6% here so that means I probably won't be getting another job anytime soon.[18]

We conducted formal pilot research on *Layoff* in 2010, and found that that the players did the following:

1. Players read the character biographies and made decisions about who to "fire" with reference to the biographies. This is verification that players understood the point of the game and engaged with its values in the way that we intended.

2. In postplay discussion, they discussed the economic crisis in terms of personal stories of people who suffered in the crisis rather than in terms of abstract economic concepts. This is also verification that they engaged with the game's values (specifically, empathy) in the way that we intended and verification that the game encouraged a particular empathy-focused way of thinking about the crisis.

3. They donated more money from their remuneration to an organization that helps people who are living in poverty. This is verification that the game, when played "empathetically," affected players' behavior.[19]

The evidence indicates that when given controversial topics and intensely charged values such as empathy, conscientious designers can communicate the nuances of values at play in a digital game. The verification process indicated that the value of empathy had been successfully implemented.

Darfur Is Dying: **Values of Leadership and Empathy** The connection of *Darfur Is Dying* (Susana Ruiz 2005) to empathy is active in the game's narrative premise, characters, player choices, context of play, and rules for interacting with nonplayable characters and the environment. Researchers investigated the influence of the game on players' willingness to offer humanitarian aid. In two different online experiments, playing *Darfur Is Dying* made a difference. In the first experiment, those who played the game reported a greater willingness to help the Darfurian people than did those who had simply read a text conveying the same information. In the second experiment, some participants watched the game, and others played it. Results indicated that playing the game, rather than observing it as a kind of animation, resulted in greater willingness to help as compared to game watching and text reading.[20]

The news media's reporting on *Darfur Is Dying* led to a Darfur Digital Activist campaign, where players could "Take Action to Stop the Crisis in Darfur" by signing petitions and taking other actions. Students, typically from the United States, were funded to travel to the Sudan to understand the genocide crisis more fully. The game creation team and publisher MTVu promoted the social awareness campaign for several years after the game's release.[21]

Verification for Designers

This chapter describes a few of the ways that designers can verify that values are embodied in games, and what designers mean when they say that values are embodied in a game. As with discovery and implementation components, we draw on game elements (including narrative premise, player choices, environments, actions, and playable characters) as the structure for verification exercises. Various studies and methods are available, based on the specific outcomes that are of interest.

Verification remains more elusive and challenging than the other two core components of the Values at Play heuristic—discovery and implementation. Nevertheless, we have seen success when verification is structured around three questions: "Is the game eliciting the right sorts of feelings?," "What attitude or behavior has changed among players, and do these changes match the game's values?," and "Is the game making players more creative, collaborative, and autonomous?"

When people ask what games can do, we can look to *Re-mission* and other health-related games that have affirmed the values of healthcare and autonomy. The Stanford study, using a staged water spill and paper towels, verified the values of sustainability and environmentalism. *Re:Mission* supported better health among players. From less successful instances, such as the activist game where extrinsic and intrinsic rewards did not match, we also learn what to avoid. *POX* spread the values of collaboration, community, and health. *Layoff* elicited particular affective responses about fairness and empathy.

More rigorous work is needed, particularly studies that test the widely varying claims for what games do well and how they do it. For example, more experimental studies are needed that focus on the effects of each game element in a given game. We need to understand better how the digital medium contributes to a game's meaning and values and what values are inherent in the games and simulations that are intended to be objective models of natural systems. A first step to taking responsibility for the values in game design is to shed the idea that games can be objective, neutral, or value free and recognize that values may enter from diverse directions and design decisions.

Individual designers may be committed but significant impact will be possible *only* if key game industry actors also adopt a role in developing not only increasingly addictive and financially rewarding games, but also games that foster a rich array of benefits with an eye to improving quality-of-life for players and others. We look to a future in which teams bravely set out values as design aspirations and verify these throughout the design process, prioritizing values as sites for innovation and solidarity. After nearly a decade of investigating values across design processes, our aspiration for the Values at Play heuristic is a pragmatic approach to making new, unique, and engaging games that also enrich the world.

III   Values at Play at Work

8 Inspiring Designers

The Values at Play heuristic—discovery, implementation, and verification—provides practical guidance for conscientious designers. It might seem daunting in the abstract, but many design teams and students have put it to work to great effect.

In addition to the theory and heuristic of Values at Play, our team has developed a curriculum that introduces value-conscious game design to graduate and undergraduate design students.[1] The curriculum includes video interviews with game designers, exercises, a recommended reading list, and discussion guides. The games discussed are those that infuse values into games, such those discussed in this book, and in particular those encountered as part of our own practice, such as *Layoff* (Tiltfactor 2009) and *POX: Save the People* (Tiltfactor 2011). Finally, *Grow-a-Game* (Tiltfactor 2007, 2008) cards have been developed to help designers brainstorm ideas for new games. *Grow-a-Game* for iPhones and iPads are able to reach design teams across technologies.

This chapter shows how these materials, individually and in combination, can inspire designers to create better games. We take a close look at aspects of the curriculum and then illustrate how the *Grow-a-Game* cards can spark creativity among design students.

Materials and Resources

Our team has created online resources that instructors and students may use in design classrooms,[2] These resources include provocative video interviews with game designers, researchers, and teachers and recommended readings by philosophers of technology, science and technology scholars, architects, and designers (game, product, and software designers).

At the core of the online resources is the curriculum, a fifty-five-page instruction guide to teaching about values in game design. It was initially developed for a four-week unit for high school or college-age students, but is used today by a variety of designers and thinkers curious about the real world implications for values in game design. These materials have been used in some form or another for years in top game design classrooms across the United States. The curriculum can be used outside the classroom by anyone wishing to think about values in ongoing design efforts. We also studied the efficacy of this material in prompting new designs, the findings of which are discussed later in this chapter.

Grow-a-Game

Grow-a-Game is a brainstorming tool that helps designers incorporate human values into their designs (figure 8.1). The *Grow-a-Game* cards can trigger conversations, ideation, and prototyping and help both novices and experts shift out of familiar thought habits. Like any good game, *Grow-a-Game* has evolved through numerous iterations of discovery, implementation, and verification in workshops, conferences, and game design courses and in consultation with our advisers, peer designers, and those who regularly use the decks.[3]

A deck of *Grow-a-Game* cards contains 86 cards in four categories or suits:

• *Values*: Each card lists a value, such as trust, privacy, liberty, or sustainability.

Figure 8.1
The *Grow-a-Game* card categories (Tiltfactor 2007).

• *Verbs*: Each card lists a game-related mechanic in the form of a verb, such as leading, building, matching, avoiding, or nurturing.

• *Games*: Each card names a familiar game that can be modified. These can be sports like football, street or analog games like hopscotch or *Monopoly*, early arcade games like *Pac-Man* (Namco 1980), or computer games like *Civilization* (Microprose 1991) or *World of Goo* (2D Boy 2008). (In the expert version of the *Grow-a-Game* deck, Game Cards are replaced with Environment Cards that specify a setting such as underwater or silent world.)

• *Challenges*: Each card names a problematic social issue such as displacement, poverty, global warming, racism, or urban sprawl.

Ways to Use *Grow-a-Game* Cards

The *Grow-a-Game* cards include instructions, but they adapt easily to various contexts and aims, such as triggering new ways to understand existing games, generating creative modifications, and building new games from scratch. Typically, the cards are used in pairs or groups. To begin a discussion of values in existing games, a small group of participants draws a values card and discusses its manifestations in existing games. Inevitably, the group has to define the value for itself (such as tradition, trust, or freedom) and hash out various interpretations of the word. Discussing a value in relation to existing games can be enlightening; often, players discover that games they assumed were value-neutral are charged with social, moral, and political dimensions.

In taking a practical turn, groups brainstorm game modifications (mods). Teams choose a game card and discuss how a given value (such as collaboration) could be used to modify an existing game, such as *Pac-Man* (Namco 1980) (figure 8.2). As they considered what might make *Pac-Man* collaborative, participants examine narrative, game mechanics, player goals, and other elements. Values conflicts result if, for example, they choose the value of peace and decide to create a first-person shooter where players gun down anyone who might be perceived to threaten world peace.

Adding further design constraints, players also might choose a game verb card and social issue card, adding these constraints to the existing constraints so that the team can experiment with iteration and inventing new games. Advanced designers tend to use game verbs and values to invent entirely new mechanics; thus the advanced card deck removes the game examples for modding and instead offers atmospheres to provide random inventive settings for these new mechanics.

Developing a Reflective Design Process

by Tracy Fullerton, Associate Professor and Electronic Arts Endowed Chair in Interactive Entertainment, University of Southern California

Over the past fifteen years, I have worked with hundreds of game design students to help them foster their ability to conceive and develop original game play. Most of these students come to my class with strong ideas about what makes a good game and what kinds of play they want to create. Part of my job is to break through these assumptions and encourage students to think in more personal, generative ways about their own design process and the potential outcomes of that process. Design instruction is as much about creating habits of mind as it is about creating aesthetic artifacts. If students cannot reflect meaningfully on their own process at the end of a game design exercise, I consider that a failure, regardless of the quality of their projects.

Over the past several years, the *Grow-a-Game* cards from the Values at Play initiative have become one of the core tools in my teaching repertoire, but I'll be honest: I have never used the cards exactly as designed. Perhaps it is because I love making up new rule variations myself, but the moment that I printed out the original version of the cards, I knew how I wanted to use them as design prompts in my class. I read the suggested rules that came with them, but based on knowing my students and the ways that they would respond to the cards, I use them in a custom way.

Back in 2005, my coinstructor, Peter Brinson, and I developed an intermediate game design class. During the fifteen-week semester, ten teams of two students each created a small but innovative and polished two-dimensional game and then launched it online.

At first, we found that mentoring these teams was a real challenge, but by 2007, we had identified useful project milestones down to a science. We knew how to get the teams moving right out of the gate and how to spot struggling teams early. We knew when to intervene with partnership counseling, scoping exercises, or implementation support. Like clockwork, the students churned out complete games with interesting formal twists.

But we also felt that students were in a rut. Peter and I wanted more from them in terms of design. Really, we wanted them to want more from *themselves* as designers. We wanted our students to develop a capacity for reflective self-critique that is crucial to any exceptional design process.

When I received an invitation to participate in the alpha test of the Values at Play curriculum, our project schedule was so tight that we could not use the entire curriculum, but we assigned several key readings in the first two weeks and added the *Grow-a-Game* cards into our ideation exercises. It created an immediate and noticeable difference in that first class. Suddenly, instead of games that had clever variations on platforming and puzzle mechanics, we had students pitching games that interrogated the democratic process, explored small human moments, and tackled large global conflicts. Once again, it became a challenge to mentor these games—not because of schedule or tools but because our students' design processes were energized with questions of meaningfulness, intent, consequence, and passion.

The intermediate students at the University of Southern California know game history, and they know mechanics. Creating variations on existing mechanics is a well-understood and much-practiced method for initiating a design process. The goal this time, however, was to engage students in a discussion that bridged game design with the humanities, philosophy, history, cultural critique, and more. We wanted to challenge them to look for sources of play in real-world conflicts, exchanges, and disequilibrium. These are tough discussions to dive into, and that is where the randomization and creative prompting that were offered by the *Grow-a-Game* cards worked well. Since that first session, I have used the cards many times in a variety of design situations involving participants ranging from middle-school students to university professors, from beginning design students to professionals with years of experience.

Since the first time that I used *Grow-a-Game*, I've liked to begin with the values cards. Everyone draws a card, and I start by giving an example of the kind of discussion that I expect from the group about the values they have drawn. Let's say I draw integrity as a value, I might begin by saying that to me, integrity involves adhering to a code of ethics, especially when people are tempted or tested, and that this code becomes a key part of defining oneself. Integrity demands work and conscious effort. Then I open up the discussion by inviting students to join in a conversation about integrity and its potential as the root of an interactive design. Someone in the group might argue that integrity does not emerge as a conscious value before it is tested. The idea that integrity must be tested raises the possibility of conflict—something that a game can be built around. Another student might share a personal story about someone who exhibits integrity. Often students will reference characters from films or games that exhibit the value. We might talk about how a particular situation brings out integrity in the form of a difficult option or how characters who are not law-abiding may still have their own brand of integrity.

Once the group has a handle on the kind of deep dive that I want them to do, I ask for volunteers to lead discussions of the values cards that they have chosen. Everyone in the room might not participate, but enough will do so to get everyone thinking about how each concept has potential tensions, references, mechanics, and play associated with it. This part of the process can't be cut short: It's the essence of what makes the exercise unique. Getting into a group discussion about the complexities of human values and how they are expressed in our own experiences, in media, in culture, and in play is what sets this brainstorming process apart from a simple random word-prompt exercise.

After we have had good discussions around several randomly chosen values, we each draw a verb card. The *Grow-a-Game* deck includes game reference cards that encourage students to think about how to mod well-known game systems using the value cards. I do not want my students to think this way about their designs, though, so I go straight to the verbs and make them work out the game play themselves. Because I usually do this exercise in classes for graduate students or intermediate-level undergraduates, I assume that students do not need a lecture on how verbs can prompt the design of original play mechanics.

Getting to good game play from verbs is not a direct process. The first ideas that come to mind when presented with a random verb are often too literal. They might make a funny pitch, but they don't really get to the full potential of the prompt. Also, verbs in game systems are often used metaphorically: we click to mean "jump" just as we click to mean "build." The meaning is created by the context and the outcome of each click within a particular system. In order to build gameplay from verbs, we first need to build a meaningful context for those verbs and a metaphoric or physical manifestation of them with which the player will engage.

During the first intermediate class in which we used the *Grow-a-Game* cards, one game concept attracted my attention. The students had drawn the value human rights and the verb *singing*. At first they were at a loss and asked to change their verb, but I encouraged them not to worry about coming up with a perfect idea. As they dug deeper into their discussion of human rights, they hit upon some cultural and media references that spoke to them and allowed them to integrate the verb *singing* in a way that transformed their simple beat-matching mechanic into an emotionally charged gameplay situation.

The idea was for a game called *Hush* (Jamie Antonisse and Devon Johnson 2007) in which the player took on the role of a mother singing a lullaby to quiet her child during a raid in the Rwandan genocide. Players sing by pressing the letters of the words of the lullaby in time with their appearance on screen. If players get out of sync, the child cries, and this alerts the soldiers outside the character's home. The more the child cries, the closer the soldiers approach. Only by singing in time can the player quiet the child and cause the soldiers to move away. The students wrote that their goal in developing this idea was to make a game in which "the player isn't viewing this horrific event from a distance and attempting to 'solve the problem.' They're in the middle of it, experiencing the terror of a Hutu raid. It's also important that even though the player is not in a position to be heroic, they still have a noble goal: Saving a child."

At first, the game concept generated heated class discussion, and students considered switching to another idea for their semester project. But Peter and I encouraged them to work out the issues that had been pointed out and to focus on their goal of illuminating this moment of personal heroism or tragedy through game play. During the class's fifteen-week development cycle, we held several sets of formal play tests in our usability lab. At the first *Hush* playtests, players had a wide range of responses. Although the usability issues with the game play were fairly standard, some players were unnerved by the premise. It became clear that students needed to clarify the tone and intent of their game—to craft both its expression of values in play and the play itself.

The team used the comments that they received to polish these integrated design elements, focusing on the arc of the player experience. They introduced a tutorial that clarified both the dramatic situation and the game interface. They honed the feedback cycle to establish a tighter sense of consequence for the player, and they added a conclusion that gave the player a sense of the broader context for this specific incident. At the end of the development process, they reflected on the game they had made: "Games typically immerse their players in fantasies of 'empowerment,' but we thought that, in this case, it would be important for the player to experience the life of a 'disempowered' person.... In *Hush*, you have very limited control over the events around you. As the mother, you must watch out your window as the violence escalates: Not only can you not stop it; you can't even take the time to react. You have to continue singing if you want to keep your baby from crying. It's a tense, anxiety-producing experience, but hopefully players come away with new empathy for the victims and survivors of the Rwandan genocide."

Having students reflect meaningfully on their own work is an important part of design instruction. With *Hush* and with many other cases that I've seen, the *Grow-a-Game* cards gave the students the impetus to involve values in their design process and also provided them with a context for evaluating what they had accomplished. It's not the cards themselves that are important. The cards simply create focal points for the design process and foster discussion around those focal points. This generates not only original ideas but reflection on these ideas—reflection that moves beyond the game-play possibilities of these ideas and into their cultural positioning and expressive potential.

Designing new mechanics is a difficult thing. Designing new mechanics that embody difficult experiences and concepts is even harder. But in my experience, game design students of all ages and experience levels are more than up to the challenge. They are, in fact, invigorated by it. It is encouraging and exciting to see these designers striving to express themselves in the development of unique game mechanics and developing the habits of mind that lead to a reflective design process.

Figure 8.2
The *Grow-a-Game* cards used in a workshop setting with Jesper Juul, Kellee Santiago, Tracy Fullerton, Staffan Bjork, Doug Thomas, and other play enthusiasts.

The *Grow-a-Game* paper decks and digital versions include more than sixty value cards. Although the cards include commonly agreed on human values (such as justice, equality under the law, individual freedom, and human rights), we recognize that the set reflects the cultural perspectives of its authors. Values such as sustainability and environmentalism also are featured because of clear expressions of interest by the design community and the public. We anticipate that values on the cards will continue to be developed to reflect cultural contexts and the interests of designers and users.

The system is adaptive. For example, existing value cards can be swapped out in favor of others that are more suited to local social, cultural, religious, geographical, or linguistic customs. Adaptations involving divergent sets of salient values or divergent meanings of those values, may even engage practices and everyday life within a single local culture, as we see, for example, in a values modification of a London Underground map (figure 8.3). Blank cards included with each *Grow-a-Game* deck allow users to modify their decks by adding values and games that reflect their own groups and world-views.

After the Values at Play curriculum had been in use for about a year, we interviewed participating instructors about their experiences.[4] Faculty

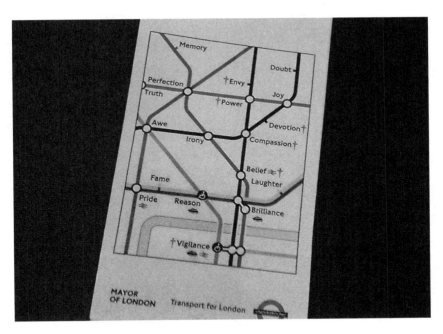

Figure 8.3
Versions of the published London Tube map have toyed with values.

members noted that the process greatly affected the student's design skills. Students were more eager to debate about design, more interested in developing novel mechanics, and less compelled to replicate the games that they had already played.

One instructor in the United States recounted a particular lesson. Someone in his class drew the humility value card, which felt particularly meaningful to his students. Humility is a thorny value in the context of games because most games position the player to be increasingly powerful, not humble. It is fun to role-play as a brainy detective, powerful warrior, or other hero, singlehandedly fighting the bad guys. This is a general game industry approach that is taken by large companies like Blizzard, which seek to make players feel more and more powerful. Game designer Rob Pardo has noted this emphasis on scale and size in games: "If something happened in the past, it happened 10,000 years ago. What's the point of having someone 8 feet tall? Just go for it."[5] Taking things to an exaggerated level in terms of distance, power, height and strength has been an accepted value in the design of many games. A value like humility seems to turn that premise upside down.

Playing (and Designing) with Values through Board Game Modification

by Celia Pearce, Associate Professor in the School of Literature, Media, and Communication, Georgia Institute of Technology

The board game has been a ubiquitous cultural form for centuries. Many of them are simplified analog simulations of real-world systems with rules that convey causal relationships between actions and outcomes. Because for centuries board games were essentially folk games, the way they evolved over time provides insight into shifts in culture. In her brilliant feminist history of chess, *The Birth of the Chess Queen* (2005), Marilyn Yalom describes the evolution of the queen piece into the most powerful piece on the board, able to move any distance in any direction. It was not accidental that this new role for the queen emerged during the reign of Queen Isabella of Spain, a woman who played an instrumental role in the age of discovery and exploration.[a]

Once the industrial age took hold, board games became mass-produced commodities that expressed the values of certain historical moments. The first board game to be published in the United States, *Mansion of Happiness* (1843), modeled Christian values as the path to a happy life. At the start of the twentieth century, there was a decided shift from moral lessons to games that touted capitalism, including games such as *Pit* (Parker Brothers, 1904).[b]

The canonical narrative in this history is the creation of *Monopoly*, which got its start as *The Landlord's Game*, and was the first board game to earn a patent. Created by Lizzie Magie, it was based on the theories of the radical economist Henry George and designed to demonstrate how the rental system enriched landlords and impoverished tenants. After failing to obtain a publishing deal, Magie repatented and self-published the game in various forms through the early 1930s. At the same time, a number of folk variants emerged, one of which was set in Atlantic City. A man named Charles Darrow further modified this variant, selling a variation at a Philadelphia department store, and eventually sold the rights to Parker Brothers, which subsequently bought Magie's patents and those of all other derivatives in order to squelch competition.[c] *Monopoly* is now the world's most successful mass-produced board game, with sales of over 275 million units worldwide.[d]

The history of *Monopoly* highlights two aspects of game design. First, game mechanics can be used to express ideas. Magie had a specific agenda—indeed, a specific ideology—in mind when she designed the *Landlord's Game*, and the same was true of many of her predecessors and contemporaries in the board game industry. The story of *Monopoly* also demonstrates how malleable games are and how easy it is to alter their values. I teach a class called "Game Design as Cultural Practice" at Georgia Tech, and each year I have my students play both the original *Landlord's Game* (I use a game-size print-out of the original patent) and the standard form of *Monopoly*. The students invariably conclude that, while the *Landlord's Game* makes its point fairly well through its game mechanics, *Monopoly* is much more fun to play. As some of them have pointed out, "It's more fun to be the bad guy." Playing these two variants of the game helps my students understand how game modification can change what values are at play.

This exercise involves two historical variants of the same game, but the same lessons can be taught through board game modification—tweaking the rules of existing games either before or even during play. My initial foray into this method took place at the 2005 Digital Games Research Association conference in Vancouver, where the women's game collective Ludica led a workshop in which participants were provided with a variety of different boards and pieces and were asked to design new games from existing, though decontextualized, pieces.[e]

The exercise was highly successful, although we had not yet engaged with the values aspect of the method.[f] Soon, however, Tracy Fullerton and I—we were among Ludica's cofounders—were invited to be on the Values at Play advisory board, and I began to incorporate the question of values into modification exercises.

At this time I was working with a group of students at Georgia Tech's Experimental Game Lab, who had formed a special-interest group called Playology. They met on a regular basis to play and critique various games, including both board and video games. Our first attempt at values-based board game modding was "Have/Have-Not Monopoly."[g]

The game arose out of an idea I had to explore the fundamental basis of capitalism—the possession of capital. After several false starts with fairly complex rule changes, we finally settled on a simple tweak: Each player had two pieces, a "have" piece and a "have-not" piece. The "have" piece played the game by the regular rules of *Monopoly*. The "have-not" piece played by the same rules, with two exceptions: it started the game with $100 instead of the usual $1500, and it received a smaller stipend when passing Go. The fate of the "have-nots" demonstrated just how important initial capital is to eventual success.

Once, as we were playing the game, one of the "have-not" pieces landed on Baltic Avenue. Because the player had not yet depleted his $100 in starting capital, he was able to purchase the property and occupy it with a building. Within a few rounds, the player had accrued some additional funds through rents on his investment. Later in the game, though, he pulled a Community Chest card that required him to pay hospital fees. As he did not have enough cash to pay the bill, he was forced to mortgage his only property. (This gaming exercise took place in the spring of 2007, a few months before the real estate market crash and the start of the economic downturn. Subsequent events, in which hundreds of thousands of people lost their jobs and homes under the burden of debt, made this gaming scenario seem somewhat prophetic.)

In the fall of 2007, Ludica joined with Mary Flanagan to develop a variant of its 2005 board game modding workshop, integrating Values at Play into the process. The workshop took place at the Digital Games Research 2007 conference in Tokyo. The objective of this exercise was to tweak the rules of existing board games and analyze the values of those games. The two games we experimented with were *Pit*, the classic Parker Brothers card game of stock trading, and *The Settlers of Catan* (1995), designed by German board game designer Klaus Teuber and published by Mayfair Games, which has become a worldwide sensation and has also been produced as an online game. The game features a reconfigurable board comprised of hexagonal tiles that represent an island. The main theme of the game is expansion. Players try to take over the board by collecting resources and building roads and structures. The only piece on the board when players arrive is the "robber," a kind of wildcard piece that is played only when the number 7 is rolled by any player. The person who rolls a 7 uses the robber piece to take resources from the other players.

Settlers of Catan seemed paradigmatic of a popular trend toward games promoting colonialism. Many video games, including the early classics *Civilization* (MicroProse 1991) and the later *Age of Empires* (Ensemble Studios, 1997), have been based on imperialist and colonialist themes. We felt a board game with this theme provided an interesting subject for examining values in games.

The workshop participants discussed the irony that the "robber" piece was colored black, which arguably could be seen as a metaphor for the indigenous peoples of Catan. One of the workshop participants decided to activate the "robber" into a player-controlled character who operated by a different set of rules from the other players. The robber's main role was to interfere with attempts by the other players to colonize the islands.

These new versions of *Monopoly* and *Settlers of Catan*, despite all their differences, shared an important quality: Both called into question the concept of symmetry, which is one of the most fundamental tenets of game design. Nearly all games provide identical starting conditions for all players, a way to ensure fairness. (A rare exception is *Risk* [Parker Brothers, 1957], in which players start with armies of different sizes controlling varying amounts of territory.) The "Have/Have-Not Monopoly" slightly subverted the concept of symmetrical starting conditions, and *Settlers of Catan* modification completely upended this concept by creating not only asymmetry but also different rules for one player. Both exercises highlighted how certain systems may favor some actors over others and how different sets of actors might also be playing by a different set of rules—either subtly, as in the reduced capital of the "have-not" pieces, or more obviously, as with the robber in the *Settlers of Catan* modification.

These game modifications also serve to critique a fundamental value of almost all games: the notion of fairness. Games, after all, often mimic systems—capitalism, colonialism—in the real world. Game rules founded on fairness suggest that the systems the games represent also are inherently fair. As these two examples illustrate, however, most real-world systems are in fact not fair to all participants. By changing game mechanics, values-driven game design can provide a powerful means to illustrate this unfairness.

Notes

a. Marilyn Yalom (2005).

b. Philip E. Orbanes (2003).

c. Orbanes (1999, 2006); Ralph Anspach (2000).

d. Retrieved July 3, 2011, from Parker Bros. website, at http://www.hasbro.com/monopoly/en_US/discover/75-Years-Young.cfm.

e. Ludica was founded in 2005 by Janine Fron, Tracy Fullerton, Jacquelyn Ford More, and Celia Pearce. For more info visit http://www.ludica.org.uk.

f. Later Fullerton and I would serve as pilot users for what would become the *Grow-a-Game* cards. The examples provided in this essay, however, were conducted prior to the development of the cards, which have since been integrated into the process by allowing participants to draw random cards from the deck to guide the modification process.

g. The Playology group was led by two of my students: Clara Fernandez, at that time a digital media Ph.D. candidate who went on to become a designer for the MIT Gambit Lab and a professor at NYU; and John Swisshelm, an undergraduate in computational media who became a professional game designer, first at Electronic Arts and later at Naughty Dog. Also participating was Matthew Weiss, a graduate of MIT who also went on to work at the Gambit Lab.

Using the *Grow-a-Game* card humility as inspiration, student designers discussed the Sony PlayStation game *Shadow of the Colossus* (Sony Computer Entertainment 2005), a beautiful, critically recognized, and unusual game with an inspired design (figure 8.4). The playable character, a warrior named Wander, begs a spiritual figure to revive a dead girl. The spirit will do so only if Wander can kill sixteen Colossi. These beautiful beasts are large, slow-moving hybrids of biological and architectural features. Some students said that when they first discovered a Colossus, they simply wanted to admire the creature and that this fascination was stronger than the game-standard imperative to attack. This is an unusual reaction to an "enemy" in any digital game. The only way for the game to move forward, however, is for Wander to attack. But when a Colossus is killed, the death scene feels tragic, not victorious, because the Colossi are not wicked creatures. After the killing, the "hero" of the game literally becomes a shadow of himself, growing thin and malevolent looking. The killing of the Colossi also releases an evil, powerful spirit from its imprisonment. Although the game at first seems to fit into the simplistic save-the-princess genre, it is ultimately a more troubling game in which winning is commingled with losing on a much grander scale.

For these students, *Shadow of the Colossus* expressed the value of humility because the protagonist's goal (save the woman) turns out to be detrimental to the security of the world. Players, who are left with the hollow feeling that their killing did not serve a just cause, realize that fighting for love does not always mean one is fighting for good. This realization takes humility.

The *Grow-a-Game* cards as a discussion starter had a deep effect on the students, as their appreciation of the idea of values, not only as a constraint,

Figure 8.4
A scene from *Shadow of the Colossus* (Sony Computer Entertainment 2005).

but as a source of innovation, took hold. This was unlike typical novice designers, who tend to fit their projects into rigid (some teachers might say "tired") genres and play conventions that are borrowed from their favorite games. After engaging in conversations that were generated by the *Grow-a-Game* cards, and with the care of a good teacher, many of these students chose to work with difficult values such as open-mindedness and dignity. The students' pursuit of the values that they cared about allowed them to leave behind mainstream conventions and create original, inventive, and meaningful designs.[6]

Revisiting the Conscientious Designer

A growing number of designers wish to make a change in their practice. Some have asked about the traits of a conscientious designer are, and how the Values at Play project can contribute to professional practice in the design studio and the world. Although *Grow-a-Game* can help start conversations about particular design challenges, it comes down to individual designers pausing to reflect on their core values and those that are behind their projects That, too, is just a start if conscientious designers hope to affect the outcome of a large design effort with inputs from many other, diverse sources.[7]

Through the course of our work we've observed that the best designers are both passionate about design and also deeply concerned about values, yet they often can't find a place for these values in the design studio. In our view, the separation of values from practice starts early: instructors and employers generally do not ask designers to be responsible decision makers. The computer science or design curriculum from which games' designers and makers emerge often do not adequately prepare students to think critically about the design process, particularly in matters of society or culture. Unless they are inspired by personal circumstances, practicing designers often feel that it is not their business to meddle with lofty ideas like human values. Values are like "philosophical stuff," unrelated to the pragmatic, time-tested patterns on which game designers rely. Yet using *Grow-a-Game* to work with students who are beginning to explore values in design can show how designers can support values while also innovating.

Through our work, we have discovered to our delight that thinking about values actually leads to more innovative ideas. Bringing the foundational aspects of the human condition to the design studio simply helps designers make dynamic, interesting games and feel good about them.

A Brief Participatory Intervention for Understanding Values at Play

by Karen Schrier, Assistant Professor, Media Arts Department, Marist College

Games, like all designed systems, devices, artifacts, media, or other products of society, embody values.[a] Analyzing the design of games, like other artifacts, gives insight into our own humanity—it helps us reflect on what it means to be human and participate in a society.[b] Examining the game design process can potentially help us take a step back and better understand our own constructed human experience.

My approach to these issues is inspired in part by the Values at Play curriculum, as well as by my own research and design practice at the intersection of ethics and gaming.[c] It has been then further honed by my interactions with college students, who have shared with me their challenges in grappling with the concept that games are *designed* systems, in which social, cultural, political values are embedded and "conveyed through design features."[d]

One primary challenge is the lack of transparency in the design process. The components of a game, like the mechanical workings of a car's engine, are hidden away. This phenomenon is not unique to games but is characteristic of many types of mediated experiences. In fact, a lack of transparency may even be necessary in that it goes hand-in-hand with a participant's willingness to suspend her disbelief. In other words, to fully immerse ourselves in a mediated experience, we may need to ignore the fact that it has been designed.[e] When students do not consider that designers create games, it follows that they may be less likely to consider how those designers and their values, biases, contexts, "beliefs and commitments and ethnic, economic, and disciplinary training and education, may frame their perspectives, preferences, and design tendencies, resulting, eventually, in features that affect the values embodied in particular systems."[f]

Another challenge is students' diverse experiences with games and widely varying definitions of a game. Some students express that they have played popular board games such as *Monopoly* (Parker Brothers, 1934) or chess. Others define *Grand Theft Auto* (Rockstar 1997) or *Call of Duty* (Activision 2003) as games but somehow exclude Hopscotch and Solitaire from this category. Still others will volunteer that they regularly play *Plants vs. Zombies* (PopCap Games 2009) or *Words with Friends* (Zynga 2009b) on their mobile devices but don't consider these to be games. Furthermore, when asked what students think of when they hear "values and gaming" or "ethics and gaming," most students cite game addiction, violence, or sexism and mention specific games such as the *Fallout* (Interplay 1997), *Mass Effect* (Microsoft Game Studios 2007), or the *Bioshock* (Irrational Games 2007) series, failing to consider that "values are always conveyed in games, through their conventional rhetorical features (e.g., story), and through their mechanics or rules."[8] In other words, values are also expressed "procedurally."[h]

To address these challenges, I designed *Trade Off*, a nondigital participatory game and reflection exercise. I have led sessions of the game in eight distinct classrooms at five different colleges in the mid-Atlantic region, with audiences ranging in size from 20 to 200 students. The game is simple, free, flexible, and transparent. It can be explained in a minute and played in about ten minutes.

Here's how *Trade Off* is played. First, I gather three piles of distinct objects from my home—about 10 to 75 units of each object, depending on the number of students. I have used paper clips, animal stickers, erasers, Legos, large beads, and coins. Once when I was on the road, I grabbed three distinct stacks of brochures I found in a hotel lobby.

Next, I prepare the classroom for the game. I make sure that all of the students are in a series of rows. If there are extra chairs or gaps between students, I fill in them in by moving students from less populated rows. I try to make the rows as compact as possible. I then randomly distribute the objects to the audience—each person gets only one of the three objects.

I then explain the basic rules: Participants are allowed to trade their objects with their neighbors immediately to the right, left, in front, or behind. In the first round, participants can also decide to hold onto their object and not trade it. There is one goal: to be a member of the first horizontal row of students to all have the same type of object.

After just a few minutes of organized chaos, one row emerges as the winner. They typically cheer and raise their object in solidarity, whether it is an animal sticker, blue bead, or snowman eraser.

In the second round of *Trade Off*, I change one rule as well as the goal. This time, participants can still trade with their immediate neighbors, but they cannot decide to hold onto their object. Instead, they need to continue switching objects, similar to "hot potato," but they cannot keep switching with the same neighbor. For example, once a student switches with a neighbor to her right, she has to switch with a neighbor to her back, left, or front next. There's also a new goal. Did the row with the animal stickers win in the first round? Well, now the goal is to *not* end up with the animal sticker when I randomly call "stop." After a few minutes of scrambled trades, I call the round and ask those participants who end up with the animal stickers to raise their hands. Instead of cheers, this time the participants stuck with the stickers are often dismayed.

After the second round of *Trade Off*, I ask the students to reflect on the differences and similarities between the two rounds. This reflective process is an integral step not only from a pedagogical perspective[i] but also as part of the "Discovery" phase in the Values at Play methodology, where designers and players "discover that certain values are relevant" to a game.[j] During this process, I guide the students as they look under the hood of *Trade Off*, and explore my design process and the resulting play experience—the trade-offs I made in developing the game, as well the behaviors, interactions, and "values that emerge through the specification of design features,"[k] or through the play of the game.

For example, during the initial reflection period, students often observed that in the first round, the students in each row collaborated as a team. They formulated, deliberated, and tested different trading strategies; negotiated with other rows or "teams"; and planned moves. In the second round, however, the students noticed a very different play style, one that was much more individualistically competitive.

In round two, students noticed that other behaviors also emerged, including cheating and secrecy. Despite a rule that participants need to keep trading, some participants held onto their non-animal sticker or refused to trade with participants who held the animal sticker. Those with an animal sticker sometimes resorted to hiding their object in the palm of their hand until the trade was complete, leaving an unpleasant surprise in their neighbor's hand. Many of those who ended up with the animal sticker in the second round explained that they felt helpless and ashamed, even if they had won the former round with that same sticker.

The game experience in the first round was akin to that of what sociologists of social networks might call a *Gemeinschaft* community, characterized by cooperation and caring. In the second round it shifted to a *Gesellschaft* community, one characterized by individualism and corruption. Thus, particular behaviors and values emerged or were rewarded based on the use of one rule or goal versus another.

The students also observed a difference in how they viewed the objects they traded. In the first round, each object was of equal value, until the team decided which object to collect. In the second round, one of the objects was arbitrarily devalued due to the rule change. The purpose of this contrast is to move the conversation away from questions of whether animal stickers, blue beads, or any other objects, are inherently better or worse, and to show how a game's system, through its design, assigns a value to an object, and that this affects what we value when we play the game.

Finally, I pose this question to the students: What would happen if we altered other aspects of the game's design? For instance, how would values be embodied and conveyed differently if the objects we traded had been photos of people we knew? What if instead of beads and animal stickers, we traded photos of fellow classmates or employees? What if in the first round, the participants needed to collect all classmates with the same first initial, the same hair color, or the same ethnicity? What would happen in the second round, when one initial, hair color or ethnicity would be suddenly verboten? While the rule change would directly affect the value of that particular category within the boundaries of the game's "magic circle," would it also affect its value outside of the game?

Although I doubt any *Trade Off* participants are now biased against animal stickers, the question helps illustrate how games, like any other systems—political, cultural, social—can assign arbitrary value to different constructs (whether a fashion item, social behavior, or technological practice), which in turn affects how those living within the system perceive and interact with those constructs. Thus, through this reflection process, the students initiate a discourse on values in games, as well as on greater social systems.

Finally, and importantly, the students realize that I did not have to design *Trade Off* this way, and there are an almost infinite number of other ways I could have designed this system. To further emphasize this concept, after initial reflections on *Trade Off*, I ask the students to co-create new permutations of the game. This relates to step two in the Values at Play methodology: that of beginning to "translate those values into design features"[l] and using this to shape the experience of the game. For example, students offered suggestions for subsequent rounds: They assigned differential points to the objects; they required rows to collect sets of objects rather than one object; they required anyone caught holding onto an object for more than a few seconds to be removed from the game; or they gave extra bonuses to those participants in the end of a row, since they observed that they had (unfairly) fewer potential trading partners.

For each of the new rules, goals, or mechanics, the students did not only discuss the possible trade-offs in values but also they *experienced* them by playing *Trade Off* with the new rules. This adheres to step three in the Values at Play methodology: testing the design translation process to iteratively "verify whether the values content of the game is as intended."[m] Likewise, after each round of iterative[n] co-design, participants reflected again on how they interacted differently based on the rule, how the balance of values was shifted, or what values the new rules, and subsequent play experiences, embodied. Since the game moves at a quick pace, it was crucial to have time for reflection between rounds in that it gave students a chance to consider, sometimes in hindsight, what they did not have time to process during game play. For example, after playing a round of *Trade Off* with the new rule that holding onto an object for too long resulted in expulsion, students noticed that the act of trading quickly became more valuable than thinking through trading strategies. They also observed that they felt more anxious because they couldn't always find someone to switch with them immediately. Some students also realized that they could get someone removed—particularly those on the ends of a row—by blocking them from trading with others and intentionally avoiding trading with them. Thus, new interactions and values emerged with yet another slight rule change.

The entire process, including introduction to the concept, game play of "Trade Off," and iterative designs and reflective practices, typically lasted 60 to 90 minutes in total.

My goal is that students who participate in *Trade Off* will begin to approach play and design differently. Concomitantly, the hope is that, first, participants will lift the hood of subsequent games and explore how values are embodied in its design and play; second, students will feel more empowered to design their own games and will iteratively reflect on how their own perspectives, biases, and values are embodied in its design and play. Third, they will begin to explore how all designed systems embody values. Games, and other designed experiences, may provide a necessary window into how other systems, such as cultural or political systems, can also affect how we interact with other people and institutions, or value certain objects, roles, or behaviors differently from others.

Notes

a. Mary Flanagan et al. (2005b, 2007).
b. Karen Schrier (2011b).
c. Values at Play Team (2007); Karen Schrier and David Gibson (2010, 2011); Schrier, 2011a.
d. Values at Play Team (2007).
e. Henry Jenkins et al. (2006); Schrier (2005).
f. Values at Play Team (2007).
g. Values at Play Team (2007).
h. Ian Bogost (2007).
i. For example, Tony Ghaye (2011).
j. Values at Play Team (2007).
k. Values at Play Team (2007).
l. Values at Play Team (2007).
m. Values at Play Team (2007).
n. Eric Zimmerman (2003).

Conclusion

As we developed the Values at Play approach, we conducted studies, held scores of workshops, and collaborated with teachers who have applied these techniques in classrooms across the world. These teachers have modded the curriculum in a number of ways to suit their particular teaching styles, the context of the classroom, and the needs of their students. This is as it should be. Values at Play is intended to be a flexible arsenal of tools for anyone who is interested in taking and teaching values seriously.

Observing Values at Play unleash creative energy in talented designers, from newly trained to experienced veterans, convinces us that it is a resource for inducing good design in all senses of the word. Check the Values at Play website for examples of what happens when talented designers incorporate values into their work. The best evidence that Values at Play works lies in the innovative games our methods have helped produce. Let us know what you think. The cycle of iteration continues.

9 Reflections on Values at Play

We shape our tools
and thereafter our tools shape us.
—Marshall McLuhan, *Understanding Media* (2003)

Not long ago we talked to Jan,[1] a former student who now works as a level designer on AAA titles—blockbuster games with big teams and enormous budgets. He started his design career in college working on a game to help middle-school girls better engage with the sciences and has gone on to work at various companies, making popular sports games and, most recently, first-person shooters.

Jan told us that he currently was on the design team for a modern military first-person shooter. At one brainstorming session, all of the creatives—level designers, game designers, art director, and so forth—were excitedly proposing unusual changes to the battle narrative, which still seemed to them to be straightforward and boring. Jan's colleague Kyle proposed that the playable character be depicted as an African American male, still a novelty for the genre. Ideas flew back and forth as the team tried to create a back story for the character. Bart suggested that to push the player into uncomfortable territory, the player character should have to take part in a rape. The character could be under pressure from his buddies to fit in by raping a woman in front of them.

Some people on the team thought the idea was brilliantly edgy or even funny. Jan, though, was repulsed. Although he was not one of the senior members of the team, he argued that players should not have to experience the game as rapists. The fact that the character would be depicted as African American added another troublesome layer. Jan posed a number of questions to his colleagues: What does this game say about rape? That it is a rite of passage for manhood? That enemies deserve to be raped? Is this game setting the stage for cowardice or for heroism? Could a game with such a mechanic actually encourage rape in the real world? That final question brought silence to the group. "It's just a game," one colleague grumbled.

"I got rid of the all-out rape, thank God," Jan told us, "but I couldn't do anything about the hanging." The game design, which was still in progress at the time of our conversation, depicted the African American character being hanged three-quarters of the way into the game. "The idea is to shock the player and make them have to pick up the pieces, as though they were really there," Jan said. "They need to take up another role." He was deeply troubled that he was working on his components—game levels that he loved to craft—on a game that later depicted the lynching of a black man.

About six months after our initial conversation, we saw Jan at a party celebrating the game's release, and he told us more about working on the game. The design team decided to change the race of the main character and have the leader of the local militia—a group allied with the playable character—be cast as African American male instead. "The marketing people were uncomfortable with a black hero," Jan noted. But the black character was lynched by invading forces anyway: "The mo-cap had already been done." Jan pulled us aside and said in a low voice, "I wish I wasn't such a sellout. I like the game, but it could be so much better. And I feel guilty making stuff I believe is wrong."

Jan's exposure to conscientious design allowed him to ask the design team a few key questions, and he brought big-picture issues about values into the design space. His was only one voice among many, however, and although he succeeded in persuading the team to get rid of the rape, the lynching scene remained.

Jan's story sums up both the promise and limitations of Values at Play. What if more people at Jan's company had experience in analyzing the values content of games? What if everyone knew that "It's only a game" belittles the act of creating games and denies the power that they have to reflect and shape our culture? Seeing this potential to provoke more informed conversations about the world of digital games, their social significance, and technology design led us to write this book.

Can Values at Play improve the ethical standards of an industry? Bringing into relief the values in existing games is a start, but our hope is for conversation to continue in the spaces that Jan inhabited—in the classrooms, laboratories, and companies where games are being developed. As we have shown, games embody many different values. And yes, some of those values are problematic. But expanding the emerging cadre of conscientious designers is something that can happen person by person and forges an important step toward values-conscious design. The Values at

Play vocabulary and heuristic are for designers, who can be powerful agents of change.

Values at Play is a social, philosophical, and technical framework that attempts to situate and integrate values in the design process of games. Games are technological artifacts created by people whose judgments are drawn from their own social experiences and places in the world. The designers' nitty-gritty design decisions about games frame how players experience the game world, andreflect designers' conscious and unconscious considerations of values and their understanding of "how the world works." As Marshall McLuhan has written, "New technological environments are commonly cast in the molds of the preceding technology out of the sheer unawareness of their designers."[2] The time has come to become more aware.

Being aware that values are at play in games is a necessary first step. But it is not enough. The environmental artist Robert Smithson said, "When a finished work of 20th century sculpture is placed in an 18th century garden, it is absorbed by the ideal representation of the past, thus reinforcing political and social values that are no longer with us,"[3] by which he meant that our works of art are context specific and inherit values from their genre's past and their current context. The social meaning of an object can be lost, taken out of context, or taken into a new context. Digital games also refer to their own history, even with the radical changes that indie gamers bring to the gaming community and the emerging games for impact that show the variety of things that games can be and do. Unequal or unfair representation, violence, and online games' history of hate speech are now all part of that story, and to break with or build on that past requires conscious effort.[4] To be conscientious designers means to understand this history and change the object in front of us (our own game) and the culture in which it will thrive.

Taking values into consideration means accepting values as one among a number of design constraints. Based on our own experiences, the greatest need of conscientious designers has been to identify a systematic way to approach values. Game design is an iterative activity that requires design teams to make many decisions on the path from concept to completion. These decisions often involve many parties with their own interests, and prioritizing values is one way to unite these parties. Those who invest the time to think about values must work through the values discovery process, implement those values into game elements, and verify those values alongside other standards. These three activities—discovery, implementation, and verification—are employed in ideation, design, programming, and quality assurance. Software must be effective, efficient, attractive, easy to use, and bug-free, but it also should work to promote the values of the surrounding societies and cultures, including liberty, community, inclusion, equality, privacy, security, creativity, trust, and personal autonomy.

In our experiences with both professional and student audiences, we have learned that thinking about values helps designers make more introspective, more engaging, and more innovative games. Values at Play encourages designers to ask questions like the following: Can we as a community of makers—designers, programmers, writers, artists, students, teachers, marketers, managers—build better games? Will people be better off with the games that are made? Can games help us solve large problems? Can games help us be better people?

Innovation arises not simply from examining but from prioritizing the human. Thinking deeply about values helps us become aware of what is at stake in our play and games. As the Roman poet Ovid famously said, "In our play we reveal what kind of people we are."

Notes

Author's note: Any unattributed interviews in this book are recent interviews with those actively working in the U.S. games industry. Names have been changed to protect their identities as these discussions at work can be unwelcome and even hostile. It is our hope that with the help of this book, such conversations can be initiated in a more open, public manner with team members, company leadership, and other stakeholders.

Introducing Values at Play

1. Kevin McCullough (2008).

2. Fox News Channel (2008).

3. The literature on media effects reveals the limited nature of these arguments, but it is likely that most television news viewers are unfamiliar with the research on established media effects (see Baran and Davis 1995; Cantril 1971; Croteau and Hoynes 2003; Gitlin 1978; Katz and Lazarsfeld 1955; Lazarsfeld and Merton 1948). Recent meta-analyses do reveal links to video game violence with aggression and reduced empathy (see Anderson et al. 2010).

1   Groundwork for Values in Games

1. The range of choice in games and the various depths of interaction available have been subjects of inquiry for numerous scholars. Espen Aarseth (1997) talks about these complications in *Cybertext: Perspectives on Ergodic Literature*, and film scholars such as Dana Polan (2009) have claimed that modern film and television have essentially become puzzles as much as narratives. Janet Murray's (1998) well-known work on player agency provides important insights. Jesper Juul (2005) and Ian Bogost (2007) both explore the subtleties of games and their meaning.

2. Lev Manovich (2002).

3. The heightened immediacy of games is taken for granted in mainstream discourse and by many players, but the effects of player agency are not yet supported very deeply in psychological studies. There is a classic research paradigm where the subject writes an essay, makes a speech, or defends a randomly chosen argument (such as public transportation funding should be cut, or alcohol should be taxed). The act of making the argument starts an unconscious process that results in the development of a more favorable attitude toward the argument (even though the experimenter arbitrarily chose the argument, and the writer may not have agreed with the argument at the outset of the experiment). This is one of the reasons that the Communist operators of North Vietnamese prison camps forced American prisoners of war to write essays denouncing capitalism: in addition to using the writings as propaganda victories, they hoped that writing the essay might lead the POWs to endorse the position. And this is why religious leaders might ask people to say prayers even if they do not believe in God: if people repeat the words of prayers, their unconscious brain might lead them to believe those words. If we try to apply these findings to games, however, the situation becomes more complicated. If players murder innocent civilians in *Grand Theft Auto* (Rockstar Games 1997), do their unconscious brains conclude that murder is acceptable? This conclusion assumes that at some level the player confuses the video game with reality.

4. Janet Murray (1998, 143).

5. Isaiah Berlin (1991, 12).

6. Robert E. Goodin (1982).

7. Langdon Winner (1986, 22).

8. Charles Taylor (2003).

9. Ruth Benedict (1993).

10. Milton Rokeach (1973).

11. Richard L. Gorsuch (1970). See a critique of the Rokeach values in Russel A. Jones, John Sensenig, and Richard D. Ashmore (1978). See the development of the Rokeach values in Gorsuch (1970) and Valerie Braithwaite and H. G. Law (1985).

12. From these three classes, Shalom Schwartz and Wolfgang Bilsky (1987, 1990) derived eight motivational domains of values—enjoyment, security, social power, achievement, self-direction, prosocial and restrictive conformity, and maturity. They also identified two additional factors (vectors)—interests (collective or individual) and goals (terminal or instrumental) that these values serve. Comparative studies of Israeli and German subjects revealed similar relationships between the factors they had identified. In the 1990s, Schwartz and Bilsky applied their theory to data from Australia, Finland, Hong Kong, Spain, and the United States, revealing a similar set of motivational values that they further organized into these categories—self-

reliance (self-direction and maturity), self-enhancement (achievement and enjoyment), and self-other relations (security, restrictive conformity, and prosociality). A further revision by Schwartz (1994) yielded a list that includes power, achievement, hedonism, stimulation, self-direction, benevolence, tradition, conformity, universalism, security, and spirituality.

13. Embodying societal values in technology has been discussed in an influential line of work that includes Lewis Mumford's writings in the 1960s about democratic and authoritarian "technics" and Langdon Winner's "Do Artifacts Have Politics?" (1986). The works that address the politics of and in technology extend across several disciplines, including information law, philosophy of technology, science and technology studies (STS), history of science and technology, innovation studies, media studies, and computer-human interaction (CHI)/usability studies. Each of these fields has absorbed the idea in its own way, expressing it in its own vernacular and integrating it into its fundamental controversies. In science and technology studies, the research literature reflects an ongoing debate over the degree to which societal outcomes are a function of technology, are tempered by contextual factors, or are fully "socially constructed." In the philosophy of technology, the question of whether values or politics are *in* technology animates a debate of whether technical systems or devices can be said to have autonomous agency. An analogous set of concerns that divide information law scholars (in multiple ways) is whether technology is able to regulate autonomously in defiance of policy or is the instrument of and under the full control of policy. For debates in STS, see Steve Woolgar (1991), Langdon Winner (1986), Bryan Pfaffenberger (1992), Donald Mackenzie and Judy Wajcman (1985), Bruno Latour (1992), and Philip Brey (2010). For philosophy of technology, see Don Ihde (1998), Peter-Paul Verbeek (2005), Albert Borgmann (1984), and Lucas Introna (2003).

14. Proponents of values in design frequently draw on James Gibson's (1986) notion of affordance, which was popularized by Donald Norman (1989) in his work on usability. They assert or demonstrate with varying degrees of rigor that a particular technical characteristic affords a certain value—that anonymity, for example, affords greater freedom of expression than, say, full identifiability. Although much interesting work has emerged from this approach, there is more to do in developing specific case analyses and in theorizing the affordance relationship as used in this context. For more on this topic, see James Gibson (1986), Donald Norman (1989), Madeline Akrich (1992), Pippen Barr, James Noble, Robert Biddle, and Rilla Khaled (2006), Philip Brey (1997), Mary Flanagan, Daniel Howe, and Helen Nissenbaum (2005a, 2005b), Bruno Latour (1992), Donald MacKenzie and Judy Wajcman (1985), Langdon Winner (1986), and Leslie Kanes Weisman (1992).

15. Cory Knobel and Geoffrey C. Bowker (2011), Jean Camp (2002), and Batya Friedman, Peter Kahn, and Alan Borning (2006, 348–372).

16. Carl DiSalvo (2010), Paul Dourish (2001), Kirsten Boehner, Rogério DePaula, Paul Dourish, and Phoebe Sengers (2007), Philip Brey (2012), and Tyler Pace, Shaowen Bardzell, and Geoffrey Fox (2010).

17. Any such analysis into layers or into component elements (as we do in chapter 3) is always an analytical move, and for any given game (or artifact) the interdependencies are thoroughgoing and essential. See, for example, the work of Marshall McLuhan (2003) and Neil Postman (1980, 1986, 1990, 1998).

18. See Matteo Bittanti and Mary Flanagan (2003) and Flanagan (2009).

19. Jim Reilly (2011).

20. Other noteworthy research relating ethics to gaming includes Miguel Sicart's *The Ethics of Computer Games* (2009), José Zagal's essays on ethics in games (Murphy and Zagal 2011), and Karen Schrier and David Gibson's edited collections (Schrier and Gibson 2010, 2011).

21. Karen Schrier and Miguel Sicart (2010).

22. One of Donald Schön's (1984) insights is that problem solving deeply involves creativity. Another insight is that commonalities exist across a range of seemingly disparate professions, including architecture, engineering, urban planning, management, and psychotherapy (and by extension, programming and game design). Looking at design thinking habits can help us to understand the commonalities that are shared by various professional challenges.

2   Uncovering Values at Play

1. Marshall McLuhan (2003, 176).

2. The link between values and sport has been conceptualized further as a system of internal goods (values like cooperation and teamwork) and external goods (high salaries, endorsement deals, and fame). These goods can change, however, according to the player or bystander's interpretive experience of game play. For a full discussion of internal and external goods in sport, see Maartje Schermer (2008) and Alasdair MacIntyre (1985).

3. In 1966, the oldest Neolithic versions of mancala were unearthed in Jordan in the Beidha discovery. They dated from approximately 6900 BC. In 1989, the 'Ain Ghazal (Jordan) excavation dated a game board from approximately 5800 BC (Rollefson 1992). Another ancient mancala game, found in western Iran, dates from approximately 6300 to 5900 BC. Archaeologist Gary Rollefson (1992) argues that these finds prove that Neolithic people had leisure time and an interest in games of chance. Other variations of mancala around the world are known as awari, oware, warri, sungka, gebeta, qarqis, bao, pallanguli, and matara.

4. James Mielke (2005a, 2005b).

5. See, for example, the *Ico* discussion thread on Sony's PlayStation Forum (community.eu.playstatio.com) and Bernard Perron and Mark J. P. Wolf (2009, 98).

6. Edge Staff (2011).

7. The full Johan Huizinga (1955, 10) passage reads as follows: "All play moves and has its being within a play-ground marked off beforehand either materially or ideally, deliberately or as a matter of course. Just as there is no formal difference between play and ritual, so the 'consecrated spot' cannot be formally distinguished from the play-ground. The arena, the card-table, the magic circle, the temple, the stage, the screen, the tennis court, the court of justice, etc., are all in form and function play-grounds, i.e. forbidden spots, isolated, hedged round, hallowed, within which special rules obtain. All are temporary worlds within the ordinary world, dedicated to the performance of an act apart."

8. Dave Cook (2010).

9. Ibid.

10. Friedrich Nietzsche (1886).

11. Chris Kohler (2007).

12. IGN (2002).

13. Mikel Reparaz (2011).

14. Tom Cheshire (2011), "In Depth: How Rovio Made *Angry Birds* a Winner (and What's Next)," *Wired*, March 7, http://www.wired.co.uk/magazine/archive/2011/04/features/how-rovio-made-angry-birds-a-winner.

15. Facebook site for *FarmVille*, accessed September 2010. Data on peak was included in Oliver Chiang (2010). The game's predecessor, *Farm Town*, was developed in 2009 by Slashkey, also for social networks (Facebook and MySpace). The differences between the games are marginal in terms of the farming interaction and metaphors about nature.

16. Player Amitesh Mondal reached 43,035 in 2011, but the game can display only 21,560 levels. His world is highly detailed, and his score became an Internet meme. His success, however, involved exploiting the game system. See http://www.youtube.com/watch?v=fS3_5khtPNs.

17. Nick Wingfield (2011).

18. Simon Parkin (2010).

19. Ian Kerr (2010).

20. Joel Penney (2010).

3 Game Elements: The Language of Values

1. Mary Flanagan, Daniel Howe, and Helen Nissenbaum (2008).

2. Staffan Bjork and Jussi Holopainen (2005); Tracy Fullerton, Christopher Swain, and Steven Hoffman (2008).

3. For Values at Play research, see Jonathan Belman and Mary Flanagan (2010) and Jonathan Belman, Mary Flanagan, Helen Nissenbaum, and Jim Diamond (2011). Other formal approaches to detailing game design elements that inform this work include those by Staffan Bjork and Jussi Holopainen (2005), Robin Hunicke, Marc LeBlanc and Robert Zubek (2004), Fullerton et al. (2008) and Katie Salen and Eric Zimmerman (2003). So much has been written on the elements of narrative in particular that it is difficult to summarize these approaches here. More recently, David Herman (2009) discusses the cross-media basic elements of Narrative as "situatedness," "event sequencing," "worldmaking/world disruption," and "what it is like" or aesthetics/environment. In defining our game elements, we match these and use the additional affordances from our own and other researchers' game research as follows: situatedness (narrative premise, point of view, characters), event sequencing (actions in a game, player choices, strategies, scoring), world making/disruption (game map, rules for interaction with nonplayer characters, rules for interaction with the environment), and what it is like (hardware and game engine, context of play, interface, and aesthetics).

4. For more on types of empathy in games, see Jonathan Belman and Mary Flanagan (2009, 5–15).

5. Miguel Sicart (2009).

6. Ian Bogost (2007, 31).

7. For more on the New Games Movement, see Andrew Fluegelman (1976).

8. Celia Pearce, Tracy Fullerton, Janine Fron, and Jacquelyn Ford Morie (2007, 266).

9. See Muzafer (1961).

10. Pearce et al. (2007).

11. Winterfuchs, "Poll: Have You Ever Cried/Teared Up during *Journey*?," thatgamecompany Forum, April 2, 2013, http://www.thatgamecompany.com/forum/viewtopic.php?f=11&t=3105.

12. For more on reskinning as a creative and political act in games, see Mary Flanagan (2009).

13. Mike Ward (2000).

14. Several scholars have taken on "platform studies" to look at the affordances of consoles. For example, see Nick Montfort and Ian Bogost (2009).

15. Early multiplayer games (with more than two players) included the little-known Atari game *MIDI Maze*, which became *Faceball* (Bulletproof Software 1991) on the Game Boy and Super NES. *Quake* most resembles the single-player *Wolfenstein 3D* (id Software 1992) and *DOOM* (id Software 1993), which allowed four simultaneous players via a local area network. *DOOM* set a high bar for creating first-person views in games and for game violence.

16. See http://fatuglyorslutty.com and http://www.NotintheKitchenAnyMore.com.

17. NBC (2011).

18. See posts such as the one at http://www.gosugamers.net/dota/news/14990-tips-on-girl-gaming. For a more lengthy example, read Aga Aquino's post about women playing *DoTA*, where he notes that while he was documenting "adult" photographs at his Internet café job, "seven girls came in and were not out to open Facebook and play another *Zynga* monstrosity, but … of all things, *Defense of the Ancients (DOTA)*. … I was already telling myself: "OK … This is weird." I have some female friends and acquaintances who happen to be avid *DOTA* players, but why did this feel so weird for me? Yes, well I have intolerant thoughts, I admit to that, that is why I have this irrational hate for Koreans." Later he goes on to celebrate his bias, noting that "Biases are there because they make up the history of our individuality and trying to alter that is just evil." From the Lighterdarkerside blog, http://thelighterdarkerside.blogspot.com/2011/03/35-girls-who-play-dota-about-strength.html. For a first-person account of this material, see the post by "Clementine" and associated comments at http://www.tiltfactor.org/dota-2-while-female. Note that the word "harassment" is part of the gameplay tactic used in the game, often through casting spells on enemies.

19. Owen Good (2011).

20. Ibid.

21. G4 (2009).

22. Jason Ocampo (2009).

23. Gamespot (2009).

24. Willie Jefferson (2009).

25. Jim Sterling (2009).

26. Richard K. James and Burl E. Gilliland (2008, 590) notes that "Urban legend and rumor, the bane of any disaster, ran rampant in New Orleans" and that the "geography of poverty" endangers disenfranchised people who cannot financially or physically able to relocate.

4   Overview of the Heuristic

1. We are thankful to design thinkers such as Donald Schön, whose 1984 book, *The Reflective Practitioner: How Practitioners Think in Action*, offers a method for reflecting about professional decisions in action. Our team furthers such thinking by inserting values directly into the intention (design goals) process.

2. Robert O. Lewis (1992, 3).

3. Iterative design is common practice in game design. Any type of game—computer game, analog game, board game, sport, or street game—must be tested constantly to see when, how, and why it works with players. In the software development literature, see Suzanne Bødker and Kaj Grønbaek (1991), Gunter Eysenbach and Christian Köhler (2002), and Ben Shneiderman (2000). In the game design literature, see Tracy Fullerton, Christopher Swain, and Steven Hoffman (2008).

4. Eric Zimmerman (2003).

5   Discovery

1. These sources of values are not necessarily independent. They can overlap and sometimes are partially constitutive of one another.

2. The concept of key actor shares characteristics with the concept of relevant social groups in the theories of the social construction of technology that are advanced by various writers, including Wiebe E. Bijker and Trevor J. Pinch (1984) and Bijker, Thomas P. Hughes, and Pinch (1987).

3. Fred Turner (2006).

4. We choose not to reveal the designer's identity or the title of the game.

5. See *The Adventures of Josie True* (Mary Flanagan 2000) at http://www.josietrue.com.

6. This occurs in nongame contexts, as well, such as in cookie management in Web browsers. When users complained that cookies violated privacy, designers gave them increasing control, thereby promoting user autonomy.

7. The discovery of values in functional descriptions is not unique to games. Privacy and security are important features of most computer, information, and media systems. A search for "privacy" on Mozilla's *Firefox Add-on* website yields 348 results, including Click&Clean ("delete private data when Firefox closes"), PrivacySuite ("one place to protect your privacy when you go online"), and TrackMeNot ("protecting privacy in web search") (accessed July 12, 20111). A search for "security" on the same site yields 246, including NoScript ("The best security you can get in a web browser") and Webutation ("Reputation & Security, and Offensive Security Exploit

Database") (accessed July 12, 2011). In addition, software developers work on privacy-enhancing technologies (PETs) and "privacy by design" (Privacy by Design 2012). Although privacy and security are prominent in public discussions, other values also drive the design of information systems. On Google's "About Google" page, the company's mission is given as "Organize the world's information and make it universally accessible and useful" (Google 2011). Similarly, One Laptop per Child (OLPC) states that its mission is "to empower the world's poorest children through education" and "to provide each child with a rugged, low-cost, low-power, connected laptop. To this end, we have designed hardware, content and software for collaborative, joyful, and self-empowered learning. With access to this type of tool, children are engaged in their own education, and learn, share, and create together. They become connected to each other, to the world and to a brighter future." OLPC is committed to promoting equity, individual self-empowerment (a dimension of autonomy), enlightenment, education, cooperation, sharing, and learning (http:// one.laptop.org/about/mission, accessed July 17, 2011). Finally, the functional definitions of software and systems that promote computer-supported cooperative work (or groupware) often include concepts such as collaboration, civic engagement, friendship, and sociality. See, for example, Victoria Sosik, Xuan Zhao, and Dan C. Cosley (2012), Selly Farnham, David Keyes, Vicky Yuki, and Chris Tugwell (2012), Travis Kriplean, Jonathan T. Morgan, Dean Freelon, Alan Borning, and W. Lance Bennett (2012).

8. *Quest Atlantis* can be played at http://atlantisremixed.org.

9. Values are listed on the project website and are more fully described in Sacha A. Barab, Tyler Dodge, Michael K. Thomas, Craig Jackson, and Hakan Tuzun (2007).

10. Examples in Batya Friedman and Helen Nissenbaum (1996), Lucas Introna (2007), Introna and Nissenbaum (2000), Yochai Benkler and Nissenbaum (2006), and Lawrence Lessig (1999).

11. Examples include Rockstar San Diego's *Midnight Club: Street Racing*, *Midnight Club II*, *Midnight Club 3: DUB Edition*, and the *Gran Turismo* series.

12. Helen Nissenbaum (2010).

13. For discussions of the cultural meanings of gifts as acts of generosity and subtle forms of imposition, see, for example, Marcel Mauss (1954) and Renee C. Fox and Judith P. Swazey (1992).

14. Collaborators in RAPUNSEL were Jan Plass and Ken Perlin at New York University. They went on to found the Games for Learning Institute at NYU.

15. Seymour Papert (2005, 38; 1993).

16. The link between social justice and access to social goods has been drawn in social science research, including, for example, in the works of political philosophers John Rawls (1971) and Michael Walzer (1984).

6 Implementation

1. These themes are revisited in chapter 7.

2. Robert Cram (2011).

3. 360Zine (2011).

4. Patrick McGuire (2013).

5. The Angry guild was founded in 2005. See http://www.guild-angry.org.

6. James Mielke (2005a, 2005b) and Nick Suttner (2009).

7. Geoff Kaufman and Mary Flanagan (in press).

8. Isaiah Berlin (1991, 12–13).

9. For a thoughtful contemporary discussion, see Henry Richardson (1990).

10. For an excellent source for this model of decision making, see Richardson (1990), in which he proposes that ethical dilemmas can be solved by specifying the norms involved and recalibrating accordingly.

11. See Mary Flanagan and Helen Nissenbaum (2008) and Flanagan, Daniel Howe, and Nissenbaum (2008).

12. Richardson (1990).

13. Transportation Security Administration (2011).

14. Ibid.

15. See an extensive description of this at Flanagan, Howe, and Nissenbaum (2008).

16. Ibid. A player as cited in our RAPUNSEL study.

17. Jonathan Belman and Mary Flanagan (2009).

7 Verification

1. See Robert L. Glass (2000), Bruno Laurel (2001), and Marc Rettig (1994).

2. Tracy Fullerton, Christopher Swain, and Steven Hoffman (2008), Glass (2000), Laurel (2001), and Rettig (1994).

3. Bjorn Freeman-Benson and Alan Borning (2003).

4. True experimental designs follow this pattern, but they use a control group and randomly assign participants to either group. These randomized control trials are used frequently in medical fields. Comparing two groups derived from the same initial group allows researchers to see the effects of the intervention more clearly.

5. Example questions and measures are available at http://Valuesatplay.org.

6. Tom Baranowski, Richard Buday, Debbie I. Thompson, and Janice Baranowski (2008).

7. Vish B. Unnithan, W. Houser, Bo Fernhall (2006).

8. Shannon R. Siegel, Bryan L. Haddock, Andrea M. Dubois, and Linda D. Wilkin (2009).

9. Pamela M. Kato, Steve W. Cole, Andrew S. Bradlyn, and Brad H. Pollock (2008).

10. Adam Gorelick (2011).

11. Mark Lepper, D. Greene, and Richard Nisbett (1973).

12. The effect size among studies was moderate (see Edward L. Deci, Richard Koestner, and Richard M. Ryan 1999).

13. For values articulation, see Sacha A. Barab, Tyler Dodge, Michael K. Thomas, Craig Jackson, and Hakan Tuzun (2007). For curricular successes in science education, see Barab, Brianna Scott, Sinem Siyahhan, Robert Goldstone, Adam Ingram-Goble, Steven J. Zuiker, and Scott Warren (2009).

14. This game was recently played at a festival of urban games in New York.

15. Although data were not collected in this project, this compelling anecdotal descriptive evidence points to larger questions about the need for values verification in games.

16. Published in Mary Flanagan et al. (2011), from which these data are reprinted.

17. Mary Flanagan and Anna Lotko (2009).

18. As quoted in ibid.

19. Forthcoming in Jonathan Belman's dissertation, "Designing Games to Foster Empathy," New York University.

20. Wei Peng, Mira Lee, and Carrie Heeter (2010).

21. See the MTVU campaign at http://www.mtvu.com/activism/politics-activism/darfur-is-dying.

8 Inspiring Designers

1. The curriculum has been used in several leading American game design programs, including at Carnegie Mellon, Dartmouth College, Georgia Tech, Hunter College, New York University, Parsons The New School for Design, Rochester Institute of Technology, the University of California San Diego, and the University of Southern California.

2. See http://valuesatplay.org.

3. Mary Flanagan, Daniel Howe, and Helen Nissenbaum (2007).

4. This section refers to results published in Jonathan Belman, Mary Flanagan, Helen Nissenbaum, and James Patrick Diamond (2011).

5. Tom Magrino (2010).

6. Jonathan Belman and Mary Flanagan (2010).

7. Donald Schön (1984).

9   Reflections on Values at Play

1. Not his real name. He requested anonymity so that he could speak frankly about situations at work.

2. Marshall McLuhan and Barrington Nevitt (1972).

3. Robert Smithson (1996, 281).

4. Amy O'Leary (2012).

References

Aarseth, Espen J. 1997. *Cybertext: Perspectives on Ergodic Literature*. Baltimore, MD: Johns Hopkins University Press.

Akrich, Madeline. 1992. "The De-Scription of Technical Objects." In *Shaping Technology/Building Society*, ed. W. Bijker and J. Law, 205–224. Cambridge, MA: MIT Press.

Anderson, Craig A., Akiko Shibuya, Nobuko Ihori, Edward L. Swing, Brad J. Bushman, Akira Sakamoto, Hannah R. Rothstein, Muniba Saleem. 2010. "Violent Video Game Effects on Aggression, Empathy and Prosocial Behavior in Eastern and Western Countries: A Meta-Analytic Review." *Psychological Bulletin* 136 (2): 151–173.

Anspach, Ralph. 2000. *The Billion Dollar Monopoly Swindle*. 2nd ed. Bloomington, IN: Xlibris Corporation.

Aquino, Aga. 2011. "Girls Who Play DOTA: About the Strength of a Woman." Thelighter/darkerside. Accessed 19 November 2013. http://thelighterdarkerside.blogspot.com/2011/03/35-girls-who-play-dota-about-strength.html.

Barab, Sasha A., Tyler Dodge, Michael K. Thomas, Craig Jackson, and Hakan Tuzun. 2007. "Our Designs and the Social Agendas They Carry." *Journal of the Learning Sciences* 16 (2):263–305.

Barab, Sasha A., Brianna Scott, Sinem Siyahhan, Robert Goldstone, Adam Ingram-Goble, Steven J. Zuiker, and Scott Warren. 2009. "Transformational Play as a Curricular Scaffold: Using Videogames to Support Science Education." *Journal of Science Education and Technology* 18:305–320.

Baran, Stanley J., and Dennis K. Davis. 1995. "Limited Effects Theory." In *Mass Communication Theory: Foundations, Ferment, and Future*. Boston: Wadsworth.

Baranowski, Tom, Richard Buday, Debbe I. Thompson, and Janice Baranowski. 2008. "Playing for Real: Video Games and Stories for Health-Related Behavior Change." *American Journal of Preventive Medicine* 34 (1):74–82.

Barr, Pippen, James Noble, Robert Biddle, and Rilla Khaled. 2006. "From Pushing Buttons to Play and Progress: Value and Interaction in Fable." *Proceedings of the*

Seventh Australasian User Interface Conference 50, 61–68. Darlinghurst, Australia: Australian Computer Society.

Belman, Jonathan, and Mary Flanagan. 2009. "Designing Games to Foster Empathy." *Cognitive Technology* 14 (2):5–15.

Belman, Jonathan, and Mary Flanagan. 2010. "Exploring the Creative Potential of Values-Conscious Design: Students' Experiences with the VAP Curriculum." *Eludamos* 4 (1):57–67.

Belman, Jonathan, Mary Flanagan, Helen Nissenbaum, and James Patrick Diamond. 2011. "Grow-a-Game: A Tool for Values Conscious Design and Analysis of Digital Games." *Proceedings of the Digital Games Research Association (DIGRA 2011): Think Design Play*, 14–17. Hilversum, The Netherlands: DIGRA.

Benedict, Ruth. 1993. "Defense of Moral Relativism." In *Moral Philosophy: A Reader*, ed. L. P. Pojman, 21–25. Indianapolis: Hackett.

Benkler, Yochai, and Helen Nissenbaum. 2006. "Commons-Based Peer Production and Virtue." *Journal of Practical Philosophy* 14 (4):394–419.

Berlin, Isaiah. 1991. *The Crooked Timber of Humanity: Chapters in the History of Ideas*. New York: Knopf.

Bijker, Wiebe E., Thomas P. Hughes, and Trevor J. Pinch, eds. 1987. *The Social Construction of Technological Systems: New Directions in the Sociology and History of Technology*. Cambridge, MA: MIT Press.

Bijker, Wiebe E., and Trevor J. Pinch. 1984. "The Social Construction of Facts and Artefacts: Or How the Sociology of Science and the Sociology of Technology Might Benefit Each Other." *Social Studies of Science* 14:399–441.

Bittanti, Matteo, and Mary Flanagan. 2003. *The Sims: Simultudini, Simboli & Simulacri*. Milano: UNICOPLI.

Bjork, Staffan, and Jussi Holopainen. 2005. *Patterns in Game Design*. Hingham, MA: Charles River Media.

Bødker, Suzanne, and Kaj Grønbæk. 1991. "Cooperative Prototyping Studies: Users and Designers Envision a Dental Case Record System." In *Studies in Computer Supported Cooperative Work: Theory, Practice and Design*, ed. J. M. Bowers and S. D. Benford, 343–357. Amsterdam: North-Holland.

Boehner, Kirsten, Rogério DePaula, Paul Dourish, and Phoebe Sengers. 2007. "How Emotion Is Made and Measured." *International Journal of Human-Computer Studies* 65 (4): 275–291.

Bogost, Ian. 2006. *Persuasive Games: The Expressive Power of Videogames*. Cambridge, MA: MIT Press.

Borgmann, Albert. 1984. *Technology and the Character of Contemporary Life: A Philosophical Inquiry*. Chicago: University of Chicago Press.

Braithwaite, Valerie, and H. G. Law. 1985. "Structure of Human Values: Testing the Adequacy of the Rokeach Value Survey." *Journal of Personality and Social Psychology* 49:250–263.

Brey, Philip. 1997. "Philosophy of Technology Meets Social Constructivism." *Techne: Journal for the Society for Philosophy and Technology* 2 (3–4):56–80.

Brey, Philip. 2010. "Values in Technology and Disclosive Computer Ethics." In *The Cambridge Handbook of Information and Computer Ethics*, ed. L. Floridi, 41–58. Cambridge: Cambridge University Press.

Brey, Philip A. E. 2012. "Anticipatory Ethics for Emerging Technologies." *NanoEthics* 6 (1): 1–13.

Brown, S. J., D. A. Lieberman, B. A. Gemeny, Y. C. Fan, D. M. Wilson, and D. J. Pasta. 1997. "Educational Video Game for Juvenile Diabetes: Results of a Controlled Trial." *Medical Informatics* 22 (1):77–89.

Camp, Jean. 2002. *Design for Values in DRM*. Bedford, NH: MITRE.

Cantril, Hadley. 1971. "The Invasion from Mars." In *Process and Effects of Mass Communication*, ed. Wilbur Schramm and Donald Roberts, 411–423. Champaign: University of Illinois Press.

Cheshire, Tom. 2011. "In Depth: How Rovio Made *Angry Birds* a Winner (and What's Next)." *Wired*, March 7. http://www.wired.co.uk/magazine/archive/2011/04/features/how-rovio-made-angry-birds-a-winner. Accessed on October 20, 2013.

Chiang, Oliver. 2010. "*FarmVille* Players Down 25% since Peak, Now below 60 Million." *Forbes*, October 15. http://www.forbes.com/sites/oliverchiang/2010/10/15/farmville-players-down-25-since-peak-now-below-60-million. Accessed on January 7, 2012.

Clark, David D., David P. Reed, and Jerome H. Saltzer. 1984. "End-to-End Arguments in Systems Design." *ACM Transactions on Computer Systems (TOCS)* 2 (4):277–288.

Cook, Dave. 2010. "Interview: *Flower*'s Jenova Chen." *NowGamer.com*, August 11. http://www.nowgamer.com/features/895327/interview_flowers_jenova_chen.html. Accessed on July 7, 2012.

Cram, Robert. 2011. "Homefront Interview with Kaos Studios." *MSXboxWorld*, March 28. http://www.msxbox-world.com/interviews/539/homefront-interview-with-kaos-studios.html. Accessed on July 13, 2012.

Croteau, David, and William Hoynes. 2003. *Media/Society: Industries, Images and Audiences*. 3rd ed. Thousand Oaks, CA: Pine Forge Press.

Deci, Edward L., Richard Koestner, and Richard M. Ryan. 1999. "A Meta-Analytic Review of Experiments Examining the Effects of Extrinsic Rewards on Intrinsic Motivation." *Psychological Bulletin* 125:627–666.

DiSalvo, Carl, Phoebe Sengers, and Hrönn Brynjarsdóttir. 2010. "Mapping the Landscape of Sustainable HCI." *Proceedings of the SIGCHI Conference on Human Factors in Computing Systems.* New York: ACM.

Dourish, Paul. 2001. "Seeking a Foundation for Context-aware Computing." *Human–Computer Interaction* 16 (2–4): 229–241.

Edge Staff. 2011. "Places: Ico's Castle." *Edge*, October 20. http://www.edge-online.com/features/places-icos-castle. Accessed on February 7, 2012.

Eysenbach, Gunter, and Christian Köhler. 2002. "How Do Consumers Search for and Appraise Health Information on the World Wide Web? Qualitative Study Using Focus Groups, Usability Tests, and In-Depth Interviews." *British Medical Journal* 324 (7337): 573–577. http://bmj.bmjjournals.com/cgi/content/full/324/7337/573. Accessed on February 12, 2005.

FarmVille Art. 2009. *FarmVille Art.* http://www.farmvilleart.com. Accessed on June 6, 2012.

Farnham, Shelly, David Keyes, Vicky Yuki, and Chris Tugwell. 2012. "Puget Sound Off: Fostering Youth Civic Engagement through Citizen Journalism." *Proceedings of the Fifteenth ACM Conference on Computer-Supported Cooperative Work (CSCW '12),* Seattle.

Flanagan, Mary. 2009. *Critical Play: Radical Game Design.* Cambridge, MA: MIT Press.

Flanagan, Mary, Daniel Howe, and Helen Nissenbaum. 2005a. "New Design Methods for Activist Gaming." *Proceedings of the Digital Games Research Association (DIGRA 2005),* Vancouver, Canada, June 16–20.

Flanagan, Mary, Daniel Howe, and Helen Nissenbaum. 2005b. "Values at Play: Design Tradeoffs in Socially Oriented Game Design." *Proceedings of CHI 2005,* 751–760. New York: ACM Press.

Flanagan, Mary, Daniel Howe, and Helen Nissenbaum. 2007. "New Design Methods for Activist Gaming." In *Worlds in Play: International Perspectives on Digital Games Research,* ed. Suzanne de Castell and Jennifer Jensen, 241–248. New York: Peter Lang.

Flanagan, Mary, Daniel Howe, and Helen Nissenbaum. 2008. "Embodying Values in Technology: Theory and Practice." In *Information Technology and Moral Philosophy,* ed. Jeroen van den Hoven and John Weckert, 322–353. Cambridge: Cambridge University Press.

Flanagan, Mary, and Anna Lotko. 2009. "Anxiety, Openness and Activist Games: A Case Study for Critical Play." *Proceedings of the Digital Games Research Association (DIGRA 2009)*, Uxbridge, UK August 31–September 4.

Flanagan, Mary, and Helen Nissenbaum. 2008. "Design Heuristics for Activist Games." In *Beyond Barbie to Mortal Kombat: New Perspectives on Gender and Computer Games*, ed. Y. B. Kafai, J. Denner, C. Heeter, and J. Sun, 265–279. Cambridge, MA: MIT Press.

Flanagan, Mary, Max Seidman, Jonathan Belman, Sukdith Punjasthitkul, Zara Downs, Mike Ayoob, Alicia Driscoll, and Martin Downs. 2011. "Preventing a *POX* among the People? Community-based Game Design for 'Herd Immunity.'" In *Proceedings of the Digital Games Research Association (DIGRA 2011): Think Design Play*, 14–17. Hilversum, The Netherlands: DIGRA.

Fluegelman, Andrew. 1976. *The New Games Book*. Garden City, NY: Dolphin.

Fox, Renee Claire, and Judith P. Swazey. 1992. *The Courage to Fail: A Social View of Organ Transplants and Dialysis*. Piscataway, NJ: Transaction.

Fox News Channel. 2008. "Fox News Mass Effect Sex Debate." *The Live News with Martha MacCullum*. January 21. http://www.youtube.com/watch?v=PKzF173GqTU. Accessed on May 16, 2012.

Freeman-Benson, Bjorn, and Alan Borning. 2003. "YP and Urban Simulation: Applying an Agile Programming Methodology in a Politically Tempestuous Domain." In *Proceedings of the 2003 Agile Development Conference*. http://dl.acm.org/citation .cfm?id=942829.

Friedman, Batya, Peter Kahn, and Alan Borning. 2006. "Value Sensitive Design and Information Systems." In *Human-Computer Interaction in Management Information Systems: Foundations*, ed. Ben Shneiderman, P. Zhang, and D. Galletta, 348–372. New York: Sharpe.

Friedman, Batya, and Helen Nissenbaum. 1996. "Bias in Computer Systems." *ACM Transactions on Information Systems* 14 (3):330–347.

Fullerton, Tracy, Christopher Swain, and Steven Hoffman. 2008. *Game Design Workshop: A Playcentric Approach to Creating Innovative Games*. Amsterdam: Elsevier Morgan Kaufmann.

Gamespot. 2009. "*Left 4 Dead 2* Interview: Chet Faliszek." *Gamespot*, June 3. http:// www.gamespot.com/left-4-dead-2/videos/left-4-dead-2-interview-chet-faliszek -6211469. Accessed on May 14, 2012.

G4. 2009. "*Left 4 Dead 2* Level Designer Interview." G4, October 28. http://www. g4tv.com/videos/42304/left-4-dead-2-level-designer-interview. Accessed on July 20, 2012.

Ghaye, Tony. 2011. *Teaching and Learning through Critical Reflective Practice*. New York: Routledge.

Gibson, James. 1986. "The Theory of Affordances." In *The Ecological Approach to Visual Perception*, 127–143. Hillsdale, NJ: Erlbaum.

Gitlin, Todd. 1978. "Media Sociology: The Dominant Paradigm." *Theory and Society* 6 (2):205–253.

Glass, Robert L. 2000. *Facts and Fallacies of Software Engineering*. Lebanon, IN: Addison-Wesley Professional.

Goodin, Robert E. 1982. *Political Theory and Public Policy*. Chicago: University of Chicago.

Good, Owen. 2011. "Well, That's One Way to Combat Misogyny in Gaming." *Kotaku*. 23 July 2011. http://kotaku.com/5824084/well-thats-one-way-to-combat -misogyny-in-gaming. Accessed November 2, 2013.

Google. 2011. "About Google." *Google*. http://www.google.com/about. Accessed on July 17, 2011.

Gorelick, Adam. 2011. "New Virtual Reality Research—and a New Lab—at Stanford." *Stanford Report*, April 8. http://news.stanford.edu/news/2011/april/virtual-reality -trees-040811.html. Accessed on July 18, 2012.

Gorsuch, Richard L. 1970. "Rokeach's Approach to Value Systems and Social Compassion." *Review of Religious Research* 11:139–143.

Greitemeyer, Tobias, and Silvia Osswald. 2010. "Effects of Prosocial Video Games on Prosocial Behavior." *Journal of Personality and Social Psychology* 98 (2):211–221. doi:10.1037/a0016997.

Herman, David. 2009. *Basic Elements of Narrative*. Chichester, UK: Wiley-Blackwell.

Huizinga, Johan. 1955. *Homo Ludens: A Study of the Play-Element in Culture*. Boston: Beacon Books.

Hunicke, Robin, Marc LeBlanc, and Robert Zubek. 2004. "MDA: A Formal Approach to Game Design and Game Research." In *Proceedings of the Nineteenth National Conference on Artificial Intelligence*, 1–5. Palo Alto, CA: AAAI Press.

IGN. 2002. "Beyond Good and Evil." *IGN*, May 24. http://pc.ign.com/ articles/360/360766p1.html. Accessed on February 19, 2012.

Ihde, Don. 1998. "Bodies, Virtual Bodies and Technology." In *Body and Flesh: A Philosophical Reader,* ed. Donn Welton, 349–357. Oxford: Blackwell Publishers.

Introna, Lucas. 2003. *On the Ethics of (Object) Things*. Lancaster University: The Department of Organisation, Work, and Technology.

Introna, Lucas. 2007. "Towards a Post-human Account of Socio-technical Agency (and Morality)." In *Proceedings of the Moral Agency and Technical Artefacts Scientific Workshop*, NIAS Hague.

Introna, Lucas, and Helen Nissenbaum. 2000. "Shaping the Web: Why the Politics of Search Engines Matter." *Information Society* 16 (3):1–17.

James, Richard K., and Burl E. Gilliland. 2008. *Crisis Intervention Strategies*. Belmont, CA: Brooks/Cole Thomson Learning.

Jefferson, Willie. 2009. "Racism in Video Games: The New Norm?" *Houston Chronicle Blogs*, July 14. http://blog.chron.com/gamehacks/2009/07/racism-in-video-games -the-new-norm. Accessed on July 15, 2012.

Jenkins, Henry, Katie Clinton, Ravi Purushotma, Alice Robison, and Margaret Weigel. 2006. *Confronting the Challenges of Participatory Culture: Media Education for the 21st Century*. Chicago: MacArthur Foundation.

Jones, Russell A., John Sensenig, and Richard D. Ashmore. 1978. "Systems of Values and Their Multidimensional Representations." *Multivariate Behavioral Research* 13:255–270.

Juul, Jesper. 2005. *Half-Real: Video Games between Real Rules and Fictional Worlds*. Cambridge, MA: MIT Press.

Kato, Pamela M., Steve W. Cole, Andrew S. Bradlyn, and Brad H. Pollock. 2008. "A Video Game Improves Behavioral Outcomes in Adolescents and Young Adults with Cancer: A Randomized Trial." *Pediatrics* 122 (2):e305–e317.

Katz, Elihu, and Paul Lazarsfeld. 1955. "Between Media and Mass." In *Personal Influence: The Part Played by People in the Flow of Mass Communication*, 15–25. Piscataway, NJ: Transaction.

Kaufman, Geoff, and Mary Flanagan. 2013. "Translation: Comparing the Impact of an Analog and Digital Version of a Public Health Game on Players' Perceptions, Attitudes, and Cognitions." *International Journal of Games and Computer Mediated Simulations* 5 (3): 1–9.

Kerr, Ian. 2010. "Digital Locks and the Automation of Virtue." In *"Radical Extremism" to "Balanced Copyright": Canadian Copyright and the Digital Agenda*, ed. M. Geist, 247–303. Toronto, ON: Irwin Law.

Knobel, Cory, and Geoffrey C. Bowker. 2011. "Values in Design." *Communications of the ACM* 54 (7):26–28.

Kohler, Chris. 2007. "'Jade Is Black?!': Racial Ambiguity in Games." *Wired*, February 10. http://www.wired.com/gamelife/2007/02/jades_black_rac. Accessed on February 16, 2012.

Kriplean, Travis, Jonathan T. Morgan, Dean Freelon, Alan Borning, and W. Lance Bennett. 2012. "Supporting Reflective Public Thought with ConsiderIt." In *Proceedings of the ACM 2012 Conference on Computer Supported Cooperative Work (CSCW '12)*, 265–274. New York: ACM.

Latour, Bruno. 1992. "Where Are the Missing Masses? The Sociology of a Few Mundane Artifacts." In *Shaping Technology/Building Society*, ed. Weibe E. Bijker and John Law, 225–258. Cambridge, MA: MIT Press.

Laurel, Bruno. 2001. *The Utopian Entrepreneur*. Cambridge, MA: MIT Press.

Lazarsfeld, Paul, and Robert Merton. 1948. "Mass Communication, Popular Taste, and Social Action." In *The Communication of Ideas*, ed. Lyman Bryson, 95–118. New York: Harper & Row.

Lepper, Mark R., David Green, and Richard E. Nisbett. 1973. "Undermining Children's Intrinsic Interest with Extrinsic Rewards: A Test of the Overjustification Hypothesis." *Journal of Personality and Social Psychology* 28 (1):129–137.

Lessig, Lawrence. 1999. "The Law of the Horse: What Cyberlaw Might Teach." *Harvard Law Review* 113:501–546.

Lewis, Robert O. 1992. *Independent Verification and Validation: A Life Cycle Engineering Process for Quality Software*. New York: Wiley-Interscience.

MacIntyre, Alasdair. 1985. *Whose Justice? Which Rationality?* London: Duckworth.

MacKenzie, Donald, and Judy Wajcman. 1985. *The Social Shaping of Technology*. Milton Keynes: Open University Press.

Magrino, Tom. 2010. "Blizzard's Pardo Serves Up Game Design Secret Sauce." *Gamespot*, March 11. http://www.gamespot.com/news/blizzards-pardo-serves-up-game -design-secret-sauce-6253464. Accessed on July 13, 2012.

Manovich, Lev. 2002. *The Language of New Media*. Cambridge, MA: MIT Press.

Mauss, Marcel. 1954. *The Gift*. Trans. I. I. G. Cunnison. London: Cohen and West.

McCullough, Kevin. 2008. "The 'Sex-Box' Race for President." *Townhall.com*. January 13. http://www.townhall.com/Columnists/KevinMcCullough/2008/01/13/the_sex-box_race_for_president?page=full&comments=true. Accessed on January 1, 2013.

McGuire, Patrick. 2013. "What's the Trouble with *Pipe Trouble*, the Satirical Game That's Inflamed Canada's Energy Battle?" *Vice*. http://motherboard.vice.com/blog/ the-trouble-with-pipe-trouble Accessed on October 15, 2013.

McLuhan, Marshall. 2003. *Understanding Media: The Extensions of Man*. Madison, WI: Gingko Press. Originally published in 1964.

McLuhan, Marshall, David Carson, Eric McLuhan, and Williams Kuhns. 2003. *The Book of Probes*. Corte Madera, CA: Gingko Press.

McLuhan, Marshall, and Barrington Nevitt. 1972. *Take Today: The Executive as Drop-out*. New York: Harcourt Brace Jovanovich.

Mielke, James. 2005a. "Design by Subtraction." *1UP*, October 13. http://www.1up.com/features/design-by-subtraction. Accessed on May 15, 2012.

Mielke, James. 2005b. "Shadow Talk." *1UP*, October 13. http://www.1up.com/features/shadow-talk. Accessed on May 15, 2012.

Montfort, Nick, and Ian Bogost. 2009. *Racing the Beam: The Atari Video Computer System*. Cambridge, MA: MIT Press.

Murphy, John, and José Zagal. 2011. "Videogames and the Ethics of Care." *International Journal of Gaming and Computer-Mediated Simulations (IJGCMS)* 3 (3): 69–81.

Murray, Janet Horowitz. 1998. *Hamlet on the Holodeck: The Future of Narrative in Cyberspace*. Cambridge, MA: MIT Press.

NBC. 2011. "Study Says Half of Girls in Middle School and High School Experience Sexual Harassment." *NBC News*, November 7. http://www.nbcwashington.com/news/health/Sexual-Harassment-Study-133351958.html. Accessed on July 18, 2012.

Nietzsche, Friedrich. 1966 [1886]. "Beyond Good and Evil." In *Basic Writings of Nietzsche*, ed. and trans. Walter Kaufmann. New York: Modern Library.

Nissenbaum, Helen Fay. 2010. *Privacy in Context: Technology, Policy, and the Integrity of Social Life*. Stanford, CA: Stanford Law.

Norman, Donald. 1989. *The Design of Everyday Things*. New York: Doubleday.

O'Leary, Amy. 2012. "In Virtual Play, Sex Harassment Is All Too Real." *New York Times*, August 1. http://www.nytimes.com/2012/08/02/us/sexual-harassment-in-online-gaming-stirs-anger.html. Accessed on August 7, 2012.

Ocampo, Jason. 2009. "E3 2009: *Left 4 Dead 2* Hands-On." *IGN*, June 1. http://xbox360.ign.com/articles/988/988416p1.html. Accessed on May 13, 2012.

Orbanes, Philip E. 2003. *The Game Makers: The Story of Parker Brothers from Tiddledy Winks to Trivial Pursuit*. Boston: Harvard Business Publishing.

Orbanes, Philip E. 2006. *Monopoly: The World's Most Famous Game & How it Got That Way*. Cambridge, MA: De Capo Press.

Pace, Tyler, Shaowen Bardzell, and Geoffrey Fox. 2010. "Practice-Centered e-Science: A Practice Turn Perspective on Cyberinfrastructure Design." *Proceedings of the 16th ACM International Conference on Supporting Group Work*. New York: ACM.

Papert, Seymour. 1993. *The Children's Machine: Rethinking School in the Age of the Computer*. New York: Basic Books.

Papert, Seymour. 2005. "The Challenges of IDC: What Have We Learned from Our Past? A Conversation with Seymour Papert, Marvin Minsky, and Alan Kay." *Communications of the ACM* 48 (1):35–38.

Parkin, Simon. 2010. "Catching Up with Jonathan Blow." *Gamasutra.com*. December 6. http://www.gamasutra.com/view/feature/6224/catching_up_with_jonathan_blow .php?page=3. Accessed on June 16, 2012.

Pearce, Celia, Tracy Fullerton, Janine Fron, and Jacquelyn Ford Morie. 2007. "Sustainable Play: Toward a New Games Movement for the Digital Age." *Games and Culture* 2 (3):261–278.

Peng, Wei, Mira Lee, and Carrie Heeter. 2010. "The Effects of a Serious Game on Role-Taking and Willingness to Help." *Journal of Communication* 60 (4):723–742.

Penney, Joel. 2010. "No Better Way to 'Experience' World War II: Authenticity and Ideology in the *Call of Duty* and *Medal of Honor* Player Communities." In *Joystick Soldiers: The Politics of Play in Military Video Games*, ed. Nina B. Huntemann and Matthew Thomas Payne, 191–205. New York: Routledge.

Perron, Bernard, and Mark J. P. Wolf. 2009. *The Video Game Theory Reader 2*. New York: Routledge.

Pfaffenberger, Bryan. 1992. "Technological Dramas." *Science, Technology & Human Values* 17 (3):282–312.

Pinder, Julian T. 2012. *Trouble in the Peace*. Toronto: Six Island Productions.

Polan, Dana B. 2009. *The Sopranos*. Durham, NC: Duke UP.

Postman, Neil. 1980. "The Reformed English Curriculum." In *High School 1980: The Shape of the Future in American Secondary Education*, ed. A. C. Eurich, 160–168. New York: Pitman.

Postman, Neil. 1986. *Amusing Ourselves to Death: Public Discourse in the Age of Show Business*. New York: Penguin.

Postman, Neil. 1990. "Informing Ourselves to Death." Paper presented at the meeting of the German Society for Computer Science (Gesellschaft für Informatik), sponsored by IBM-Germany, Stuttgart, October 11 1990. http://w2.eff.org/Net_culture/ Criticisms/informing_ourselves_to_death.paper. Accessed on January 7, 2014.

Postman, Neil. 1998. "Five Things We Need to Know about Technological Change." Paper presented at the conference for The New Technologies and the Human Person: Communicating the Faith in the New Millennium, Denver, Colorado, March 27. http://www.technodystopia.org. Accessed on October 3, 2012.

Privacy by Design. 2012. "About PbD." *Privacy by Design*. http://www.privacyby design.ca. Accessed on August 2, 2012.

Rawls, John. 1971. *A Theory of Justice*. Cambridge, MA: Belknap of Harvard University Press.

Reilly, Jim. 2011. "Saints Row Penetrator Altered in Japan." *GameInformer*, November 10. http://www.gameinformer.com/b/news/archive/2011/11/10/saints-row-penetrator-altered-in-japan.aspx. Accessed on May 28, 2012.

Reparaz, Mikel. 2011. "*Rayman Origins, Beyond Good & Evil* and the State of the Games Industry: An Interview with Michel Ancel." *Gamesradar*, September 29. http://www.gamesradar.com/rayman-origins-beyond-good-evil-and-state-games-industry-interview-michel-ancel/?page=2. Accessed on February 24, 2012.

Rettig, Marc. 1994. "Prototyping for Tiny Fingers." *Communications of the ACM* 37 (4):21–27.

Richardson, Henry. 1990. "Specifying Norms as a Way to Solve Concrete Ethical Problems." *Philosophy and Public Affairs* 19(4): 279–310.

Rokeach, Milton. 1973. *The Nature of Human Values*. Glencoe, IL: Free Press.

Rollefson, Gary O. 1992. "A Neolithic Game Board from 'Ain Ghazal, Jordan." *Bulletin of the American Schools of Oriental Research* 286 (May):1–3.

Salen, Katie, and Eric Zimmerman. 2003. *Rules of Play: Game Design Fundamentals*. Cambridge, MA: MIT Press.

Schell, Jesse. 2008. *The Art of Game Design: A Book of Lenses*. Burlington, MA: Elsevier.

Schermer, Maartje. 2008. "On the argument that enhancement is 'cheating.'" *Journal of Medical Ethics* 34 (2):85–88.

Schön, Donald. 1984. *The Reflective Practitioner: How Professionals Think in Action*. New York: Basic Books.

Schrier, K. 2005. "Revolutionizing History Education: Using *Reliving the Revolution (RtR)* to Teach Multiple Histories." Master's thesis, Massachusetts Institute of Technology, Cambridge, MA.

Schrier, K. 2011a. "An Investigation of Ethical Thinking in Role-Playing Video Games: A Case Study of *Fable III*." PhD diss., Columbia University, New York.

Schrier, K. 2011b. "Preface." In *Designing Games for Ethics: Models, Techniques, and Frameworks*, ed. K. Schrier and D. Gibson. Hershey, PA: IGI.

Schrier, Karen, and David Gibson, eds. 2010. *Ethics and Game Design: Teaching Values through Play*. Hershey, PA: IGI.

Schrier, Karen, and David Gibson, eds. 2011. *Designing Games for Ethics: Models, Techniques and Frameworks*. Hershey, PA: IGI.

Schrier, Karen, and Miguel Sicart. 2010. "Ethics and Game Design." Invited talk at NYU's Game Center, New York.

Schwartz, Shalom H. 1994. "Cultural Dimensions of Values: Toward an Understanding of National Differences." In *Individualism and Collectivism*, ed. Kim Uichol, Harry C. Triandis, and Gene Yoon, 85–119. London: Sage.

Schwartz, Shalom, and Wolfgang Bilsky. 1987. "Toward a Psychological Structure of Human Values." *Journal of Personality and Social Psychology* 53:550–562.

Schwartz, Shalom H., and Wolfgang Bilsky. 1990. "Toward a Theory of the Universal Content and Structure of Values: Extensions and Cross-Cultural Replications." *Journal of Personality and Social Psychology* 58:878–891.

Sherif, Muzafer, O. J. Harvey, B. Jack White, William R. Hood, and Carolyn W. Sherif. 1961. *Experimental Study of Positive and Negative Intergroup Attitudes between Experimentally Produced Groups: Robbers Cave Study*. Norman: University of Oklahoma. Originally published in 1954.

Shneiderman, Ben. 2000. "Universal Usability." *Communications of the ACM* 43 (May):84–91.

Sicart, Miguel. 2009. *The Ethics of Computer Games*. Cambridge, MA: MIT Press.

Siegel, Shannon R., Bryan L. Haddock, Andrea M. Dubois, and Linda D. Wilkin. 2009. "Active Video/Arcade Games (Exergaming) and Energy Expenditure in College Students." *International Journal of Exercise Science* 2 (3):165–174.

Sosik, Victoria, Xuan Zhao, and Dan C. Cosley. 2012. "See Friendship, Sort Of: How Conversation and Digital Traces Might Support Reflection on Friendships." In *Proceedings of the ACM Conference on Computer Supported Cooperative Work (CSCW '12)*. Seattle, Washington, February 11–15.

Smithson, Robert. 1996. *Robert Smithson: The Collected Writings*. 2nd ed. Ed. Jack Flam. Berkeley: University of California Press.

Sterling, Jim. 2009. "Valve Responds to *Left 4 Dead 2* Racism Accusations." *Destructoid*, July 30. http://www.destructoid.com/valve-responds-to-left-4-dead-2-racism-accusations-141921.phtml. Accessed on May 28, 2012.

Suttner, Nick. 2009. "Shadow of the Colossus Postmortem Interview." *1UP*, January 29. http://www.1up.com/features/shadow-colossus-postmortem-interview. Accessed on May 15, 2012.

Taylor, Charles. 2003. *Modern Social Imaginaries*. Durham, NC: Duke University Press.

Thaler, Richard H., and Cass R. Sunstein. 2008. *Nudge: Improving Decisions about Health, Wealth, and Happiness*. New Haven, CT: Yale University Press.

360Zine. 2011. "Homefront Interview." *Gamerzines*, March 17, http://www.gamerzines.com/xbox/news-xbox/homefront-interview.html. Accessed on February 19, 2012.

Transportation Security Administration. 2011a. "Advanced Imaging Technology (AIT)." *TAS: Advanced Imaging Technology (AIT).* http://www.tsa.gov/approach/tech/ait/index.shtm. Accessed on August 30, 2012.

Transportation Security Administration. 2011b. "TSA Takes Next Steps to Further Enhance Passenger Privacy." *Transportation Security Administration.* July 20. http://www.tsa.gov/press/releases/2011/0720.shtm. Accessed on September 18, 2012.

Turner, Fred. 2006. *From Counterculture to Cyberculture: Stewart Brand, the Whole Earth Network, and the Rise of Digital Utopianism.* Chicago: University of Chicago.

Unnithan, Vish B., W. Houser, and Bo Fernhall. 2006. "Evaluation of the Energy Cost of Playing a Dance Simulation Video Game in Overweight and Non-Overweight Children and Adolescents." *International Journal of Sports Medicine* 27 (10):804–809.

Values at Play Team. 2007. Values at Play: Curriculum and Teaching Guide (4-week version).

Verbeek, Peter-Paul. 2005. *What Things Do: Philosophical Reflections on Technology, Agency, and Design.* University Park: Penn State Press.

Walzer, Michael. 1984. *Spheres of Justice: A Defense of Pluralism and Equality.* New York: Basic Books.

Ward, Mike. 2000. "Being Lara Croft, or, We Are All Sci Fi." *Pop Matters,* January 14. http://popmatters.com/features/000114-ward.html. Accessed on April 4, 2012.

Weisman, Leslie Kanes. 1992. *Discrimination by Design: A Feminist Critique of the Man-Made Environment.* Urbana: University of Illinois Press.

Wingfield, Nick. 2011. "Virtual Products, Real Profits: Players Spend on Zynga's Games, but Quality Turns Some Off." *Wall Street Journal,* September 9. http://online.wsj.com/article/SB10001424053111904823804576502442835413446.html. Accessed on May 24, 2012.

Winner, Langdon. 1986. "Do Artifacts have Politics?" In *The Whale and the Reactor,* 19–39. Chicago: University of Chicago Press.

Winterfuchs. 2013. "Poll: Have You Ever Cried/Teared Up during *Journey*?" *Thatgamecompany Forum,* April 2. http://www.thatgamecompany.com/forum/viewtopic.php?f=11&t=3105. Accessed on April 2, 2013.

Woolgar, Steve. 1991. "The Turn to Technology in Social Studies of Science." *Science, Technology & Human Values* 16 (1):20–50.

Yalom, Marilyn. 2005. *Birth of the Chess Queen.* New York: Harper Collins.

Zimmerman, Eric. 2003. "Play as Research: The Iterative Design Process." *Ericzimmerman.com,* July 8. http://ericzimmerman.com/texts/Iterative_Design.html. Accessed on February 2, 2012.

Game References

Activision. 2003. *Call of Duty*. Microsoft Windows, Mac OS X, N-Gage, Xbox Live Arcade PlayStation Network. Developed by Infinity Ward.

Activision. 2007. *Call of Duty 4: Modern Warfare*. Microsoft Windows, PlayStation 3, Xbox 360, Mac OS X, Wii. Developed by Infinity Ward.

Amtex and Seta. 1998. *Tetris 64*. Nintendo 64.

Anne W. Abbott and S. B. Ives. 1843. *The Mansion of Happiness: An Instructive Moral and Entertaining Amusement*. Board game.

Area/Code. 2010. *Power Planets*. Adobe Flash.

Atari. 1973. *Gotcha*. Arcade.

Atari Inc. 1976. *Breakout*. Arcade.

Atari Inc. 1979. *Asteroids*. Arcade.

BioWare. 2003. *Star Wars: Knights of the Old Republic*. Xbox, Microsoft Windows, Mac OS X. LucasArts.

BioWare. 2007. *Mass Effect*. Xbox 360, Microsoft Windows. Microsoft Game Studios.

Black Isle Studios. 1999. *Planescape: Torment*. Microsoft Windows. Interplay Entertainment.

Blizzard Entertainment. 1994. *Warcraft: Orcs & Humans*. MS-DOS, Mac OS.

Blizzard Entertainment. 1998. *StarCraft*. Windows, Mac OS, Nintendo 64.

Blizzard Entertainment. 2004. *World of Warcraft*. Mac OS X, Microsoft Windows.

Bulletproof Software/Blue Planet Software. 1991. *Faceball 2000*. Game Boy.

Capcom. 1984. *1942*. Arcade.

Capcom Production Studio 4. 2005. *Resident Evil 4*. GameCube, PlayStation 2, Microsoft Windows, Wii, Mobile Phone, iPhone, Zeebo, iPad, PlayStation 3, Xbox 360. Capcom.

Chess. Date unknown. Indian board game.

Clover Studio. Capcom. 2006. *Okami*. PlayStation 2, Wii.

Conor O'Kane. 2008. *Harpooned*. Microsoft Windows, Mac OS X.

EA Digital Illusions CE. 2008. *Mirror's Edge*. PlayStation 3, Xbox 360, Microsoft Windows, iOS.

EA Digital Illusions CE. 2011. *Battlefield 3*. Microsoft Windows, PlayStation 3, Xbox 360, iOS.

Edgar Cayce. 1904. *Pit*. Trading card game.

Eidos. 1996. *Tomb Raider*. MS-DOS, PlayStation, Sega Saturn.

Elizabeth Magie. 1904. *The Landlord's Game*. Board game.

Elizabeth Magie, Senaria Karim, Charles Darrow. 1935. *Monopoly*. Board game. Parker Brothers.

Ensemble. 1997. *Age of Empires*. Microsoft Windows, Windows Mobile. Microsoft Game Studios.

Epic Games. 2006. *Gears of War*. Xbox 360, Microsoft Windows. Microsoft Game Studios.

Financial Entertainment. 2010. *Farm Blitz*. Adobe Flash.

Football. 1869. American sport.

Go. Date unknown. Asian board game.

Guerillapps. 2011. *Trash Tycoon*. Adobe Flash.

Harmonix Music Systems. 2011. *Dance Central 2*. Xbox 360.

Higinbotham, William. 1958. *Tennis for Two*. Analog computer/Oscilloscope.

HopeLab/Realtime Associates. 2006. *Re-Mission*. Microsoft Windows.

Hopscotch. Estimated mid-17th century. Physical game.

Hybrid Arts, Inc. 1987. *MIDI Maze*. Atari ST.

id Software. 1992. *Wolfenstein 3D*. DOS, Mac, Amiga 1200, Apple II, Acorn Archimedes, NEC PC-9801, SNES, Jaguar, GBA, 3DO, Windows Mobile, iOS, PlayStation Network, Xbox Live Arcade. Apogee Software.

id Software. 1993. *Doom*. MS-DOS, NEXTSTEP, IRIX, Solaris, Mac OS, Linux, Microsoft Windows, Acorn RISC OS, Jaguar, Sega 32X, PlayStation, SNES, 3DO, Sega Saturn, Nintendo 64, Game Boy Advance, Xbox, Xbox 360, Tapwave Zodiac, iPhone.

id Software. 1996. *Quake*. DOS, Macintosh, Sega Saturn, Nintendo 64. GT Interactive.

ImpactGames. 2007. *PeaceMaker* Mac OS X, Windows.

Infinity Ward, Treyarch, SledgehammerGames, Raven Software, Gray Matter Interactive, Pi Studios, Spark Unlimited, Amaze Entertainment, Rebellion Developments, Ideaworks Game Studio, Activision, Aspyr Media. 2003–present. *Call of Duty (series)*. Microsoft Windows, Mac OS X, Nintendo DS, GameCube, Nokia N-Gage, PlayStation 2, PlayStation 3, PlayStatiaon Portable, Wii, Xbox, Xbox 360, iOS, BlackBerry.

Interplay Entertainment, Black Isle Studios, Micro Forte, Bethesda Game Studios, Obsidian Entertainment, Masthead Studios. Interplay Entertainment, 14 Degrees East, Bethesda Softworks. 1997–present. *Fallout* (series). DOS, Microsoft Windows, Mac OS X, PlayStation 2, PlayStation 3, Xbox, Xbox 360.

Irrational Games and Looking Glass Studios. 1999. *System Shock 2*. Microsoft Windows. Electronic Arts.

Irrational Games, 2K Games. 2007–present. *Bioshock* (series). Xbox 360, PlayStation 3, Microsoft Windows.

Jamie Antonisse and Devon Johnson. 2007. *Hush*. Microsoft Windows, Mac OS X.

Kaos Studios. *Homefront*. 2011.

Klaus Teuber. 1995. *The Settlers of Catan*. Board game. Kosmos, Mayfair Games.

Konami Computer Entertainment Tokyo. 1998. *Dance Dance Revolution*. Arcade, PlayStation. Konami of America, Konami of Europe GmbH.

Lionhead Studios, Big Blue Box. 2004. *Fable*. Xbox, Xbox 360, Microsoft Windows, Mac OS X. Microsoft Game Studios.

Lionhead Studios. Activision. 2005. *The Movies*. Microsoft Windows, Mac OS X.

London Studios. 2004. *SingStar*. PlayStation 2, PlayStation 3.

Long Shot Games. 2011. *Remote Shepherd*. Microsoft Windows.

Lucasfilm. 1989. *Pipe Mania*. Amiga, Atari ST, DOS.

Mancala. Circa 6900 BC. Northern African board game.

Mary Flanagan. 2000. *The Adventures of Josie True*. Adobe Flash.

Mary Flanagan. 2006. *[giantJoystick]*. Atari, interactive sculpture.

Mary Flanagan. 2012a. *Awkward Moment*. Paper, HTML5.

Mary Flanagan. 2012b. *Buffalo*. Paper, HTML5.

Maxis. 2000. *The Sims* Microsoft Windows, Mac OS, PlayStation 2, Xbox, Game-Cube. Electronic Arts.

McKinney. 2011. *Spent*. Web.

Microsoft. 2004. *Fable*. Xbox, Xbox 360, Microsoft Windows, Mac OS X.

MicroProse. 1990. *Sid Meier's Railroad Tycoon*. DOS, Amiga, Macintosh, Atari ST.

MicroProse. 1991. *Sid Meier's Civilization*. DOS, Windows, Macintosh, Amiga, Sega Saturn, Atari ST, Super Nintendo Entertainment System, PlayStation.

Microsoft Game Studios, Electronic Arts, BioWare. 2007–present. *Mass Effect* (series). Xbox 360, Microsoft Windows, PlayStation 3, iOS.

Mojang. 2011. *Minecraft*. Java platform, Java applet, Android, iOS, Xbox 360.

Molleindustria. 2006. *The McDonald's Videogame*. Web, Adobe Flash download. http://www.mcvideogame.com.

Namco, Midway. 1980. *Pac-Man*. Arcade.

Namco, Midway. 1981. *Galaga*. Arcade.

Namco. 2004. *Katamari Damacy*. PlayStation 2.

NanaOn-Sha. 1996. *PaRappa the Rapper*. PlayStation, PlayStation Portable.

Naughty Dog. 1996. *Crash Bandicoot*. PlayStation, PlayStation Network.

Naughty Dog, SCE Bend Studio, Sony Computer Entertainment. 2007–present. *Uncharted* (series). PlayStation 3, PlayStation Vita.

Naughty Dog, Sony Computer Entertainment. 2009. *Uncharted 2: Among Thieves*. PlayStation 3.

NCsoft. 2004. *City of Heroes*. Microsoft Windows, Mac OS X. Developed by Cryptic Studios, Paragon Studios.

Nintendo Creative Department. 1985. *Super Mario Bros*. Nintendo Entertainment System.

Nintendo, Capcom/Flagship, Vanpool, Grezzo, Monolith Soft, Nintendo. 1986–present. *The Legend of Zelda* (series). Nintendo Entertainment System, Game Boy, Super Nintendo, Nintendo 64, Game Boy Color, Game Boy Advance, GameCube, Nintendo DS, Wii, DSi, 3DS.

Playdead. 2010. *Limbo*. Xbox Live Arcade, PlayStation Network, Microsoft Windows, Mac OS X. Microsoft Game Studios.

PopCap Games. 2001. *Bejeweled*. Microsoft Windows, Mac OS X, Browser, PDA, Mobile, iPod, Windows Phone, Java ME, Xbox, Facebook.

PopCap Games. 2009. *Plants vs. Zombies*. Google Chrome, Microsoft Windows, Mac OS X, iOS, Xbox Live Arcade, PlayStation Network, Nintendo DS, DSiWare, Bada, Android, Windows Phone 7, PlayStation Vita, BlackBerry Tablet OS.

Pop Sandbox. 2012. *Pipe Trouble*. Mac OS X, Android.

Powerful Robot Games. 2003. *September 12th: A Toy World*. Browser.

RAPUNSEL with NSF Support. 2006. *Peeps*. Board game.

RedOctane/Activision. 2005. *Guitar Hero*. PlayStation 2. Developed by Harmonix.

Rockstar Games. 1997–present. *Grand Theft Auto* (series). Microsoft Windows, PlayStation, Xbox, PlayStation 2, PlayStation 3, Xbox 360, Nintendo DS, iPhone.

Rovio Entertainment. 2009. *Angry Birds*, iOS, Maemo, MeeGo, HP webOS, Android, Symbian3, Series 40, PSP, PlayStation 3, Mac OS X, Windows, WebGL, Windows Phone 7, Google Plus, Google Chrome, BlackBerry Tablet OS, Bada, Facebook.

Ruth Catlow. 2001. *Rethinking Wargames: 3 Player Chess*. Adobe Flash.

Sasha Barab. 2005. *Quest Atlantis*. Microsoft Windows, Mac OS X.

Sega. 2001. *Rez*. Dreamcast, PlayStation 2.

Slashkey. 2009. *Farm Town*. Facebook, Myspace.

Sony Computer Entertainment. 1996. *Crash Bandicoot*. PlayStation, PlayStation Network. Developed by Naughty Dog.

Sony Computer Entertainment. 2001. *Ico*. PlayStation 2, PlayStation 3.

Sony Computer Entertainment. 2005. *Shadow of the Colossus*. PlayStation 2, PlayStation 3.

Square. 1995. *Chrono Trigger*. Super Nintendo, PlayStation, Nintendo DS, Mobile phones, Virtual Console, PlayStation Network, iOS.

Susana Ruiz. 2005. *Darfur Is Dying*. Browser.

Thatgamecompany. 2009. *Flower*. PlayStation 3. Sony Computer Entertainment.

Thatgamecompany. 2012. *Journey*. PlayStation 3. Sony Computer Entertainment.

The 63rd Gallon. 2011. *Tribernetica*. Microsoft Windows.

THQ. 2011a. *Deepak Chopra's Leela*. Xbox 360, Wii.

THQ. 2011b. *Homefront*. Microsoft Windows, PlayStation 3, Xbox 360.

Tiger Style. 2012. *Waking Mars*. Microsoft Windows, Mac OS X, Linux, Android, iOS.

Tiltfactor Lab and Helen Nissenbaum. 2007, 2008. *Grow-a-Game.* Card game.

Tiltfactor Lab, with the Rochester Institute of Technology (RIT) Game Design and Development program. 2008. *Profit Seed.* Adobe Flash.

Tiltfactor Lab and the Rochester Institute of Technology (RIT) Game Design and Development program. 2009. *Layoff.* Microsoft Windows.

Tiltfactor Lab. 2010. *POX: Save the People.* Board game.

Tiltfactor Lab. 2011. *POX: Save the People.* Adobe Flash and iOS.

Tiltfactor Lab. 2012. *ZOMBIEPOX.*

Turbine Entertainment Software. 1999. *Asheron's Call.* Windows.

Turbine, Inc. 2007. *The Lord of the Rings Online: Shadows of Angmar.* Microsoft Windows.

2D Boy and Nintendo. 2008. *World of Goo.* Windows, Mac OS X, Linux, iOS, WiiWare, Android.

Ubisoft. 2003. *Beyond Good & Evil.* PlayStation 2, Microsoft Windows, Xbox, Game-Cube, Xbox Live Arcade, PlayStation Network.

United Game Artists. 2001. *Rez.* Dreamcast, PlayStation 2, Xbox 360. Sega.

Valve Corporation and Sierra Entertainment. 1998. *Half-Life.* Microsoft Windows, PlayStation 2.

Valve Corporation. 2003. *Defense of the Ancients.* Mac OS, Mac OS X, Microsoft Windows. Designed by "Eul."

Valve Corporation. 2007. *Portal.* Microsoft Windows, Mac OS X, PlayStation 3, Xbox 360, Linux.

Valve Corporation. 2009. *Left 4 Dead 2.* Microsoft Windows, Xbox 360, Mac OS X.

Valve Corporation. 2011. *Portal 2.* Microsoft Windows, Mac OS X, PlayStation 3, Xbox 360.

Valve Corporation. 2012. *Dota 2.* Microsoft Windows, Mac OS X.

Volition, Inc., and THQ. 2006. *Saints Row.* Xbox 360.

Volition Inc. 2011. *Saints Row: The Third.* Microsoft Windows, PlayStation 3, Xbox 360.

WaveQuest/Raya Systems. 1995. *Packy and Marlon.* Super NES.

Zach Gage. 2011. *SpellTower.* Mac OS X, Android, IOS.

Zynga. 2009a. *FarmVille.* Adobe Flash, iOS, HTML5.

Zynga. 2009b. *Words with Friends.* Android, iOS, Facebook, Kindle Fire, Nook Tablet.

Index

DATE DUE	RETURNED
OCT 14 2015	